SCIENCE

MADE SIMPLE

Portable Press

An imprint of Printers Row Publishing Group

10350 Barnes Canyon Road, Suite 100, San Diego, CA 9212

www.portablepress.com • mail@portablepress.com

Printers Row Publishing Group is a division of Readerlink Distribution Services, LLC.
Portable Press is a registered trademark of Readerlink Distribution Services, LLC.

Correspondence regarding the content of this book should be sent to Portable Press, Editorial Department, at the above address. Author, illustration, and rights inquiries should be sent to Quarto Publishing plc, 6 Blundell Street, London, N7 9BH, www.quartoknows.com.

Portable Press

Publisher: Peter Norton • Associate Publisher: Ana Parker

Editor: JoAnn Padgett

Produced by The Bright Press, an imprint of Quarto Publishing plc

Publisher: James Evans

Editorial Director: Isheeta Mustafi

Managing Editor: Jacqui Sayers

Editors: Katie Crous and Abbie Sharman

Art Director: Katherine Radcliffe

Designers: Tall Tree and Subtract Design

Library of Congress Control Number: 2019957636

ISBN: 978-1-64517-254-3

Printed in China

24 23 22 21 20   1 2 3 4 5

Cover Design: Greg Stalley

Cover Images: Shutterstock

SCIENCE
MADE SIMPLE

A COMPLETE GUIDE IN TEN EASY LESSONS

VICTORIA WILLIAMS

PORTABLE
PRESS

San Diego, California

CONTENTS

INTRODUCTION

Why do things float? Why do we have day and night? What happens to the food you eat? Why can you see your face in a mirror? What exactly is electricity? The world is full of questions and mysteries, and people have been testing ideas to try and find the answers for thousands of years.

Some mysteries—like the five mentioned up there—have already been solved, and you will find the answers in this book. Other puzzles are still being figured out by scientists, expert mystery-solvers who carry out experiments to find new clues and possible solutions. Solving mysteries about the world is not a neat, simple process; people sometimes get things wrong, miss important clues, and discover things completely by accident. Scientists work together and use the knowledge of those that came before them to head toward the right answers. There is so much going on in the universe that we will probably never understand all of it, but we are learning all the time, and that's one of the reasons science is so exciting.

Science isn't just in books and scientists' heads—it is everywhere you look, from planes flying overhead to your dinner cooking in the oven. It has allowed us to cross oceans, light up our homes at night, and even land on the moon. In this book you'll explore space, burrow deep underground, take a journey through the human body, find out what everything (yes, everything) in the universe is made of, and much more. It would be impossible to fit everything we've found out about science into one book, but this one will explain everything a junior scientist needs to know. Once you've finished reading, it's up to you to decide which parts you want to learn more about and where your science adventure takes you next. Who knows—maybe one day you will make an important discovery and change science forever.

ABOUT THIS BOOK

This comprehensive guide of **10 lessons** (chapters) covers the key concepts of science. This book guides you methodically through this vast field, with the featured lessons offering insight into its numerous applications in the world around us. From our own planet to outer space, from ecosystems to electricity, and from motion to genes— the cornerstone discoveries, pioneering scientists, and the knowledge they have brought are shared in these pages. Throughout the book there are various features that will help guide you and deepen your understanding.

- **LESSON INTRODUCTION**
  At the start of each lesson is a handy introduction, to outline the key learning points.

FACT Most topics have an intriguing fact highlighted in an easy-to-see box.

QUIZ TIME

Find these quizzes at the end of each lesson and grade yourself on your understanding and progress before moving on to the next lesson.

SIMPLE SUMMARY

At the end of each lesson is a summary, to help you recap the topics covered.

ANSWER THIS

At the end of each topic is a spot test, which should help to assess whether you have fully understood the information on those pages and how to apply it in real-life situations. Try to answer these questions immediately after reading the relevant pages, without peeking at the text for answers.

- **ANSWERS**
  Turn to the back of the book for answers to all the Answer This and Quiz Time tests—no cheating now!

1

MATTER AND MATERIALS

Everything is made of matter, from the clothes you're wearing and the air against your skin to the stars burning in the farthest corner of outer space. Matter can be arranged in billions of different ways, creating all the different textures, colors, and smells around you.

WHAT YOU WILL LEARN

Particles and atoms

Chemical elements

The periodic table

Molecules and compounds

Properties of materials

Chemical reactions

Acids and alkalis

PARTICLES AND ATOMS

All the matter in the universe—all the "stuff" that exists, from air and dust to gold and diamond—is made up of particles called atoms. Our bodies are built of billions of tiny cells, and each cell is made of about 100 trillion atoms. Atoms are so small they can only be spotted with the most powerful microscopes in the world.

If you were able to see inside an atom, you'd notice that it contains three types of "subatomic particles": protons, neutrons, and electrons. Protons and neutrons cluster together to form a nucleus in the center, while electrons spin around the outside. Neutrons, as their name suggests, are neutral—they have no charge. Protons have a positive charge ("pro" means positive, like when you make a list of pros and cons), while electrons are negatively charged. The opposite charges attract, like magnetic poles, so the protons in the nucleus keep the electrons in their orbits. The number of each of these subatomic particles in the atom determines the element it makes (see page 14).

Electrons orbit the nucleus in "shells." These aren't solid shells like eggshells or snail shells—they're different layers of space around the nucleus, like the orbits of the planets around the Sun. Each electron shell has room for a certain number of electrons. The farther away a shell is from the center of the atom, the bigger it is and so the more electrons it can hold.

FACT

```
There are things even smaller than subatomic
particles. Neutrons and protons are made up of
miniscule particles called quarks. Quarks are so
small that it wasn't until the 1960s that scientists
even realized they existed.

It's estimated that there are more atoms in one grain
of sand than the total number of grains of sand on all
the beaches in the world; and more atoms in the human
body than all the stars in the sky.
```

ANSWER THIS

1. Which subatomic particle has a positive charge?

2. Which is smallest: proton, neutron, or electron?

3. Electrons orbit in _____ .

4. What is the center of an atom called?

5. The farther a shell is from the center, the _____ electrons it can hold.

Atoms last a very long time—usually forever. They can change form and swap electrons during chemical reactions (see page 22), but their nuclei are very hard to break apart. The atoms that make up your body were made billions of years ago, and before they came together to form you they were probably part of a dinosaur, a star, a lake, or another person.

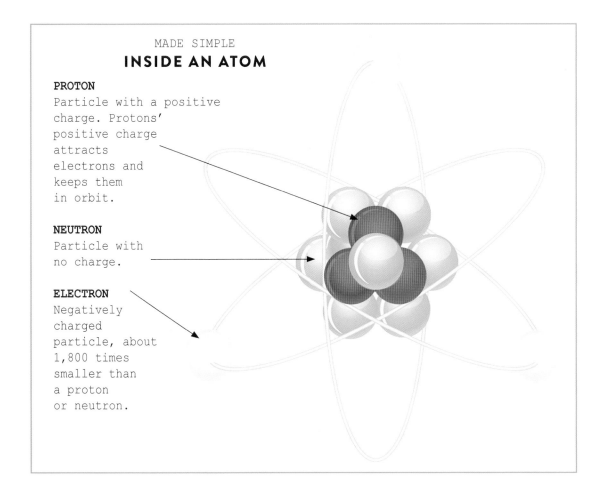

MADE SIMPLE
INSIDE AN ATOM

PROTON
Particle with a positive charge. Protons' positive charge attracts electrons and keeps them in orbit.

NEUTRON
Particle with no charge.

ELECTRON
Negatively charged particle, about 1,800 times smaller than a proton or neutron.

CHEMICAL ELEMENTS

Atoms can be made up of different numbers of protons, neutrons, and electrons. When atoms with the same structure and number of subatomic particles group together they form an element—a pure substance that can't be broken down into anything else.

Everything that exists contains the atoms of at least one element. Some elements, like helium, stay by themselves and don't combine with anything else, but most other elements can join together to form molecules.

There are over 90 elements that occur naturally. After scientists discovered atoms and found out what makes an element unique, they began to alter the number of subatomic particles to create new elements. If you include the man-made ones, there are currently 118 elements, but this number could go up as more are created.

Chemical symbols

You might have heard people saying they're "battling the elements" when the weather is bad. This is because some ancient cultures tried to explain nature using the "classical elements"—earth, water, fire, and air. Elements like oxygen, hydrogen, and silver are often referred to as "chemical elements" so it's clear that it's different atoms being talked about.

Each chemical element has its own symbol. The same symbol is used all across the world; no matter what language someone is speaking or writing in, oxygen is always O and helium is always He. Some of the symbols don't seem to match the names, like Au for gold and Fe for iron. This is because the symbol comes from a word that isn't English, usually because the element was discovered by a scientist from another country.

FACT
```
Hydrogen is the most common element in the universe.
It is one of the simplest atoms, made of a single
proton and electron. After the big bang (see page 50),
hydrogen and helium were the very first elements to form.
```

SILVER, COPPER, HELIUM, AND NEON

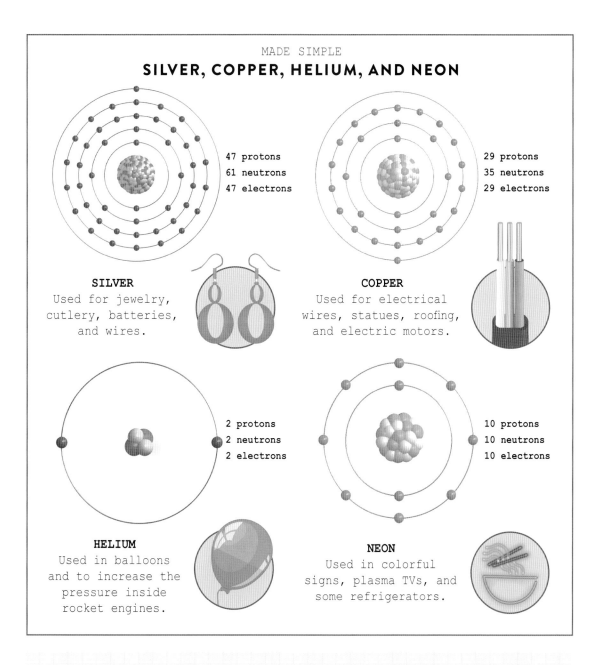

47 protons
61 neutrons
47 electrons

SILVER
Used for jewelry,
cutlery, batteries,
and wires.

29 protons
35 neutrons
29 electrons

COPPER
Used for electrical
wires, statues, roofing,
and electric motors.

2 protons
2 neutrons
2 electrons

HELIUM
Used in balloons
and to increase the
pressure inside
rocket engines.

10 protons
10 neutrons
10 electrons

NEON
Used in colorful
signs, plasma TVs, and
some refrigerators.

ANSWER THIS

1. How many naturally occurring elements are there?

2. An element can't be _____.

3. Which element can be used for TVs and signs?

4. Chemical symbols are _____ in different countries.

THE PERIODIC TABLE

First suggested in 1869 by Russian chemist Dmitri Mendeleev, the periodic table allows scientists to identify patterns and similar properties in chemical elements. It does its job so well that scientists have even been able to predict the properties of elements before they've been discovered.

All 118 chemical elements are arranged in the periodic table. This chart organizes the elements by the structure of their atoms, putting them in columns and rows known as groups and periods. Because atomic structure determines an element's properties, elements in the same group (column) often have similar properties.

GROUP

PERIOD

PERIODIC TABLE

The periodic table lists all the different elements. The lightest elements are at the top. Only about 20 elements are nonmetals.

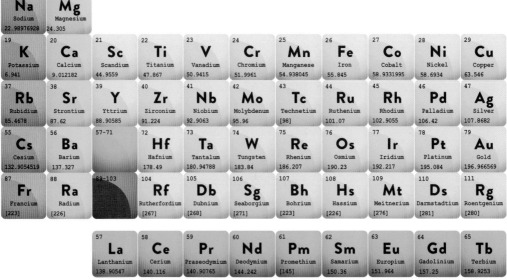

| Alkali metals | Alkaline earth metals | Transition metals | Lanthanides | Actinides | Basic metals |

Group 18 (the group farthest to the right) is the inert gases. These gases are very stable and usually don't react with other elements because all their electron shells are full.

ANSWER THIS

1. Elements in a period have the same number of _____.

2. Who first proposed the periodic table?

3. Elements in a _____ usually have similar properties.

4. Which group doesn't usually react with other elements?

5. Are there more metal or nonmetal elements?

Atomic number
Number of protons in the nucleus

Chemical symbol

Atomic mass
The mass of one atom of an element

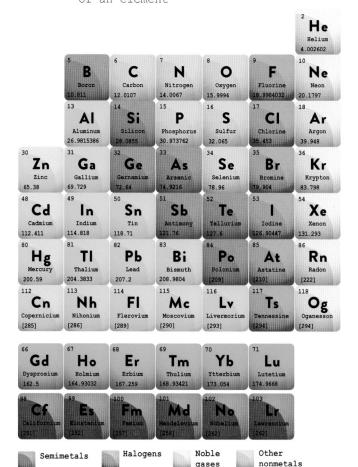

Semimetals   Halogens   Noble gases   Other nonmetals

PERIOD
All the elements in a period have the same number of electron shells around the nucleus.

GROUP
All the elements in a group have the same number of electrons in their outer shell. They often look alike and behave in similar ways.

MOLECULES AND COMPOUNDS

LESSON 1.4

A molecule is created any time two or more atoms join together. There are billions of different ways that atoms can combine. This is why there are so many different colors, textures, smells, tastes, and substances around you.

Some molecules are made up of one type of atom. Oxygen, for example, usually travels around in pairs. Most molecules, though, are compounds—molecules made up of atoms from more than one element. Water is made of molecules that each contain two hydrogen atoms and one oxygen atom.

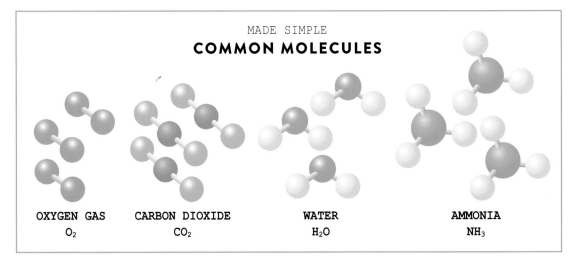

MADE SIMPLE
COMMON MOLECULES

OXYGEN GAS	CARBON DIOXIDE	WATER	AMMONIA
O_2	CO_2	H_2O	NH_3

The "ingredients" of a molecule can be written in a molecular formula. The formula lists everything in the molecule and the ratio of atoms. The formula for water is H_2O—notice how the number of atoms goes after the letter it relates to, not before. When there's no number after a letter it means there is just one atom of that type.

FACT

The smallest molecules, like molecules of oxygen gas, are made of just two atoms. Some molecules, like proteins and DNA, are made of thousands, millions, or even billions of atoms—they're known as macromolecules, and they're visible under a microscope.

Chemical bonds

Atoms in molecules are held together by chemical bonds. There are two main bonds: ionic and covalent, which both involve electrons. Electron shells want to hold the maximum number of electrons they have room for. When shells aren't full, atoms will try to bond with others to make the right number and become stable.

In covalent bonds, the atoms share some electrons so they both end up with full outer shells. These bonds are quite weak. Stronger ionic bonds are formed when one atom donates electrons to another. Atoms with only a few electrons in their outer shell give them away, while atoms with nearly full outer shells accept electrons from others to fill the gaps. When one atom gives electrons to another, they no longer have an equal number of electrons to protons. The donor atom becomes positively charged and the receiver becomes negatively charged, so they're held together by attraction.

ANSWER THIS

1. Is water a chemical element?

2. What are the two main types of chemical bond?

3. What is a compound?

4. Which type of bond is stronger?

5. All the atoms in a molecule can be written out in a _____.

COVALENT BONDS VS. IONIC BONDS

COVALENT BOND
Electrons are shared.

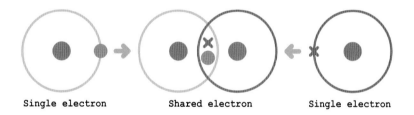

Single electron   Shared electron   Single electron

IONIC BOND
Electrons are donated from one atom to another.

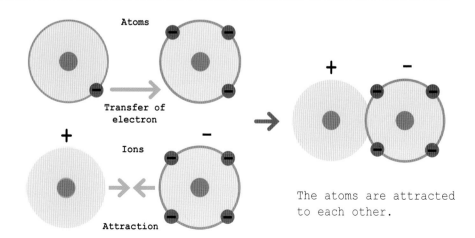

Atoms

Transfer of electron

Ions

Attraction

The atoms are attracted to each other.

PROPERTIES OF MATERIALS

A material is a substance or mixture of substances with a name such as wood, metal, plastic, rubber, and glass. The properties of a material are the features that you can measure or sense and can use to describe how it looks, feels, and behaves.

Different properties are useful for different tasks—paper is great for writing on and wrapping presents with, but you wouldn't build a house out of it.

Metal

A metal object can be made from one element or a combination of metal elements called an alloy. Most metals are hard, strong, and shiny. They conduct heat and electricity, and some are magnetic. They're malleable, ductile, and durable.

Glass

Glass is made by melting minerals together at extremely high temperatures. Thick glass is very strong, but thin glass is brittle. Glass is usually transparent, which makes it useful for glasses and windows.

Plastic

Plastics are man-made materials created by combining certain chemicals. Plastic can be made into almost any shape. It's waterproof and a good insulator of heat and electricity.

Rubber

Rubber is made from oil or a substance called latex that comes from the rubber tree. It's waterproof and highly elastic, so it is used to make a range of objects from bouncy balls to boots.

FACT

Diamond is one of the hardest natural materials on Earth. It's formed when carbon atoms are put under extreme pressure and forced very close together. Strong bonds hold the atoms in place so they can't move apart again. Diamond easily scratches and cuts through other materials, but few substances can scratch it.

MATERIALS AND THEIR PROPERTIES

Here are just some of the properties of a material that you can observe or test:

STRENGTH
How much force it
can withstand
before breaking.

TOUGHNESS
How well it can
absorb sudden
impacts.

MALLEABILITY
How easily it can
be turned into a
new shape.

ELASTICITY
How easily it
returns to its
original shape.

STIFFNESS
How resistant it
is to being bent.

DUCTILITY
How easily it can
be pulled to make
thin cables.

CONDUCTIVITY
Whether it
conducts heat or
electricity.

ABSORBENCY
Whether it
soaks up liquids
like water.

HARDNESS
Resistance to
scratching, drilling,
deformation.

BRITTLENESS
How likely it is
to shatter or
suddenly break.

DURABILITY
How well it
resists wear
and tear.

**OPACITY/
TRANSPARENCY**
Whether it lets
light through.

ANSWER THIS

1. What is absorbency?

2. Give an example of a
   brittle material.

3. Which properties make metal
   useful for electrical wires?

4. Is wood opaque or transparent?

1.6 CHEMICAL REACTIONS

Cooking food, burning fuel in cars, digesting food in your intestines, and finding that the milk has gone sour—chemical reactions don't just happen in a laboratory, they take place all around us. Reactions occur when substances interact and their atoms rearrange.

In chemical reactions, the bonds between atoms in a molecule break. The atoms separate and then come together in new combinations. Energy is transferred to or taken from the surroundings, and new substances are created. The substances that react with each other are called the reactants. The substances produced by the reaction are called the products.

MADE SIMPLE
TYPES OF REACTIONS

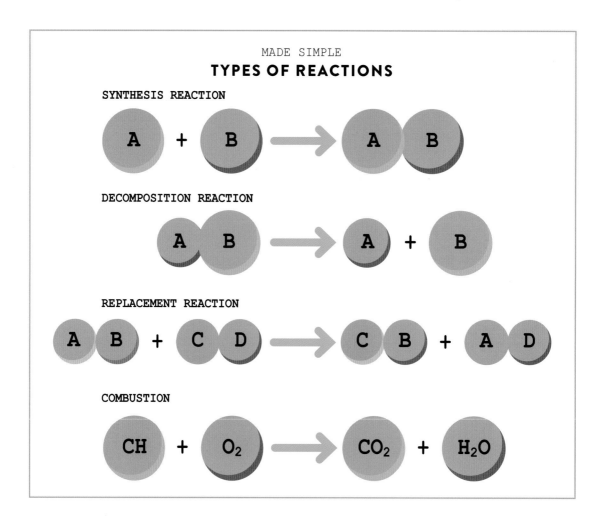

SYNTHESIS REACTION

A + B → A B

DECOMPOSITION REACTION

A B → A + B

REPLACEMENT REACTION

A B + C D → C B + A D

COMBUSTION

CH + O_2 → CO_2 + H_2O

Changes that don't involve atoms rearranging are called physical changes. When a substance melts or gets squashed it changes state or shape, but the atoms don't form different combinations or make new substances.

Although they move around and rearrange, no atoms are lost or made in a reaction; the number of atoms in the products is always the same as the number of atoms in the reactants, so the total mass is the same at the start and end of the reaction. This is called conservation of mass.

There are many different types of chemical reactions:
• **Synthesis or combination** When two or more reactants combine to make a new compound.
• **Decomposition** A reaction where a substance breaks down into several products.
• **Replacement** When one atom takes the place of another in a compound.
• **Combustion** Burning, an exothermic (heat-giving) reaction involving oxygen.

The reactants and products of a reaction can be shown in a chemical equation. The equation is written using either the names of the substances or their molecular formulas, and shows how all of the atoms rearrange. A chemical equation should always be balanced—there should be exactly the same number of atoms on each side of the arrow.

Reactions happen at different rates—paper combusts quickly, but iron rusts slowly. Catalysts are substances that speed up a reaction without being changed or used up. They are important in large industrial reactions, because the quicker a reaction takes place, the more product can be made in a day. Heating substances can also increase the speed of the reaction.

CHEMICAL EQUATION

C + O O → O C O

CARBON
C

OXYGEN GAS
O_2

CARBON DIOXIDE
CO_2

ACIDS AND ALKALIS

Almost every liquid in the world is either acidic or alkaline to some degree. Acids are sharp, and strong acids can corrode (wear away at) other substances. Alkalis are often soapy, and strongly alkaline liquids are used to get rid of grease and dirt.

Acidic liquids contain lots of hydrogen ions. Hydrogen ions are positively charged atoms that form when a water molecule loses one of its two hydrogens. They're positively charged because they have one less negative electron than a normal hydrogen atom. Hydrogen ions are represented by the symbol H^+. Alkaline liquids contains lots of hydroxide ions, the negatively charged molecules left behind when water loses a hydrogen atom. They're negatively charged because they have an extra electron. Hydroxide ions are given the symbol OH^-.

THE PH SCALE

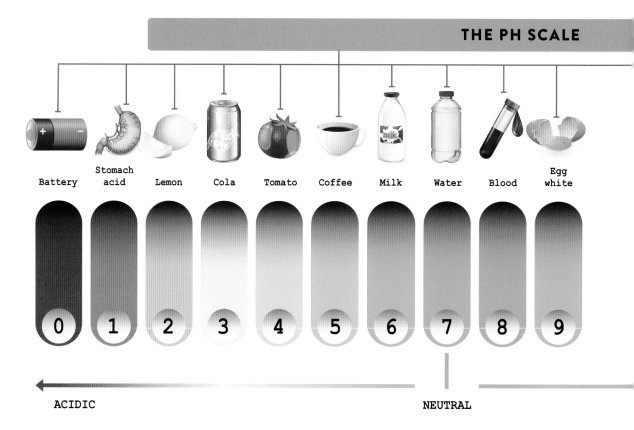

| Battery | Stomach acid | Lemon | Cola | Tomato | Coffee | Milk | Water | Blood | Egg white |

0 1 2 3 4 5 6 7 8 9

ACIDIC

NEUTRAL

The pH scale

How acidic or alkaline a substance is can be measured on a scale called the pH scale. The scale goes from 0 to 14, with 0 being very acidic and 14 being very alkaline. Substances at either end of the scale are highly reactive and can be dangerous if they're not used carefully. Weak acids have a pH of 5 or 6, and weak alkalis have a pH of 8 or 9. Substances with a pH of 7 are completely neutral—they're neither acidic nor alkaline. Neutral liquids are rare, but they include distilled (pure) water and petrol.

Neutralization

A chemical reaction takes place when you mix an acid and an alkali. It's called neutralization, because if you add the right amount of acid and alkali, the positive charge of the hydrogen ions and the negative charge of the hydroxide ions cancel each other out and the reaction produces neutral water and a salt. Neutralization is an exothermic reaction, so the mixture warms up.

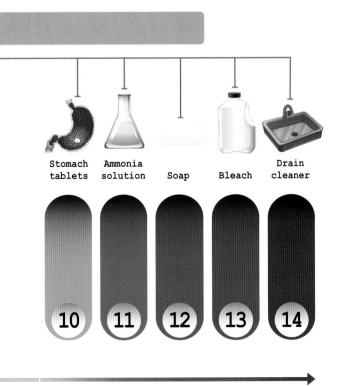

Stomach tablets   Ammonia solution   Soap   Bleach   Drain cleaner

10   11   12   13   14

ALKALINE

ANSWER THIS

1. What charge does a hydroxide ion have?

2. What are the products of neutralization reactions?

3. What has a pH of 10?

4. How do alkalis taste?

5. What is the pH of stomach acid?

MATTER AND MATERIALS

1. **What sort of charge does an electron have?**
   a. Positive
   b. Negative
   c. Magnetic
   d. Neutral

2. **Which element is diamond made of?**
   a. Neon
   b. Oxygen
   c. Carbon
   d. Nitrogen

3. **How many chemical elements are there?**
   a. 102
   b. 90
   c. 136
   d. 118

4. **Which of these words would not be used to describe a metal?**
   a. Ductile
   b. Conductive
   c. Elastic
   d. Malleable

5. **What happens in a synthesis reaction?**
   a. A substance burns
   b. One atom takes the place of another in a compound
   c. Two or more reactants combine to make a new compound
   d. A substance breaks down into several products

6. **What is absorbency?**
   a. How resistant a material is to bending
   b. How well a material soaks up liquids like water
   c. How easily a material can be shaped
   d. How long a material lasts

7. **Elements in the right-hand group (column) of the periodic table have _____ electron shells.**
   a. Full
   b. No
   c. Empty
   d. Damaged

8. **The reactants and products of a reaction can be shown using a _____.**
   a. Chemical symbol
   b. Chemical equation
   c. Chemical bond
   d. Chemical formula

9. **Acids contain lots of _____.**
   a. Hydrogen ions
   b. Water molecules
   c. Oxygen atoms
   d. Hydroxide ions

10. **What are the products of neutralization?**
    a. Water and oxygen
    b. Salt and water
    c. Hydrogen and salt
    d. Oxygen and hydrogen

Answers on page 210

SIMPLE SUMMARY

Everything is made of matter, and it can be arranged in billions of different ways, creating different textures, colors, and smells.

- All the matter in the universe is made up of particles called atoms, which contain three "subatomic particles": protons, neutrons, and electrons.

- When atoms with the same structure and number of subatomic particles group together they form an element—a pure substance that can't be broken down into anything else.

- All 118 chemical elements are arranged in the periodic table, which organizes the elements by the structure of their atoms, putting them in columns and rows known as groups and periods.

- A molecule is created any time two or more atoms join together.

- The atoms in molecules are held together by chemical bonds.

- A material is a substance or mixture of substances, such as wood, metal, plastic, rubber, and glass. The properties of a material are the features that you can measure or sense.

- In chemical reactions, the bonds between atoms in a molecule break. The atoms separate and then come together in new combinations.

- Almost every liquid in the world is either acidic or alkaline to some degree.

- How acidic or basic a substance is can be measured on a scale called the pH scale. The scale goes from 0 to 14, with 0 being very acidic and 14 being very alkaline.

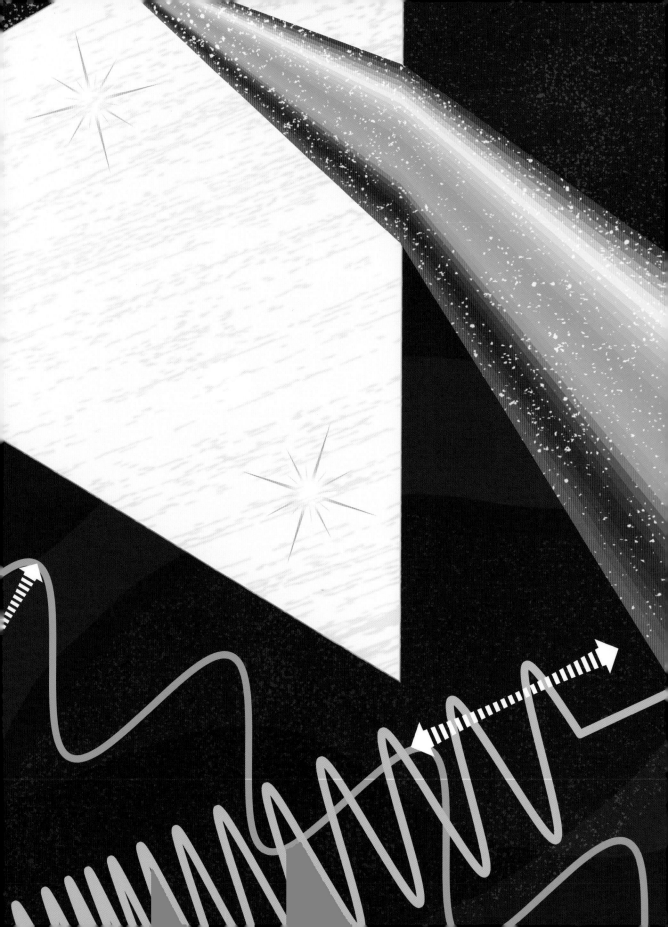

2
WAVES

Why do you see lightning before you hear thunder? How can a doctor see your bones? How does the Internet work? It's all to do with waves. In fact, it's a certain type of wave that will help you to read this next chapter…

WHAT YOU WILL LEARN

Wave properties

X-rays

The electromagnetic spectrum

Radio waves

Visible light

Sound

Color

Ultrasound and infrasound

WAVE PROPERTIES

When we hear the word "wave" our first thought is often the ocean or a friendly hello, but in physics the word describes a disturbance (vibration) that travels through space and matter and transfers energy from one place to another.

Waves are either mechanical or electromagnetic. Mechanical waves like sound waves travel by causing disturbances to a medium like air or water, whereas electromagnetic waves like light move through electrical and magnetic fields and don't need matter to keep moving. Another way to group waves is by the direction in which the disturbance travels. Transverse waves move up and down as well as transferring energy forward, like the movement of a stretched slinky if you wiggle one end up and down.

FACT

Waves on the ocean are called surface waves. They're not like transverse or longitudinal waves; they're created when wind blows over the top of the sea and makes the water at the surface move in circular motions.

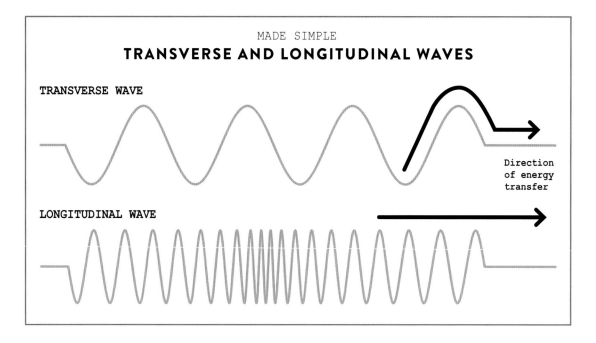

MADE SIMPLE
TRANSVERSE AND LONGITUDINAL WAVES

TRANSVERSE WAVE

Direction of energy transfer

LONGITUDINAL WAVE

PARTS OF A WAVE

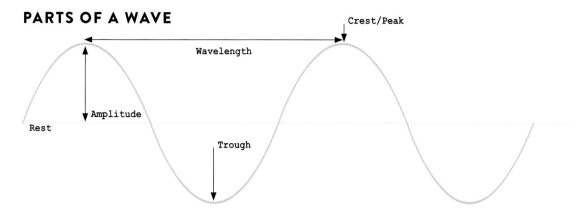

REST	PEAK	TROUGH	WAVELENGTH	AMPLITUDE
The position of the field or particle when it's not being vibrated.	The highest point above the rest position.	The lowest point below the rest position.	The length of one full wave cycle, usually measured from crest to crest.	The greatest distance from the rest position.

Now imagine you shove the end of the slinky forward. Parts will compress (bunch up) and then stretch out again as the wave moves along in the same direction as the energy—this is how a longitudinal wave travels.

Wave properties

There are five main properties of waves. Changing any one of these alters how the wave behaves and travels.

- **Amplitude** The height of the crest above the resting position, or its intensity.
- **Wavelength** The distance from crest to crest.
- **Frequency** The number of waves passing a point in one second, measured in hertz (Hz).
- **Period** The time it takes for one complete wave to pass a point.
- **Speed** How fast the disturbance is moving through space or through a medium.

As you will see in the rest of this chapter, waves are moving all around us. It's because of them that we can see and hear the world, and new discoveries have allowed people to use waves for everything from examining broken bones to cooking food.

ANSWER THIS

1. Which type of wave needs a medium to travel through?

2. What is the highest point of a wave called?

3. What is the resting position?

4. Which type of wave moves up and down as well as forward?

5. How is wavelength usually measured?

THE ELECTROMAGNETIC SPECTRUM

Electromagnetic (or EM) waves are superfast waves that can move without a medium like water or air—they can move through a vacuum. The electromagnetic spectrum arranges these waves from longest to shortest. With such a huge range of frequencies, each type of wave has its own unique uses and potential dangers.

For a long time, people only knew about visible light because this was the part of the spectrum they were able to see. All the other waves are invisible to the naked human eye, and it wasn't until fairly recently that people

THE ELECTROMAGNETIC SPECTRUM

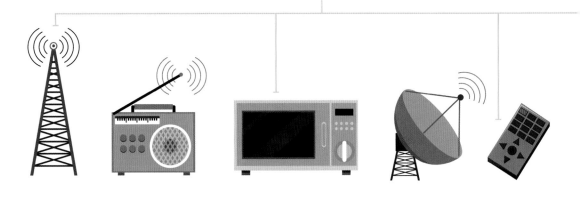

RADIO WAVES	MICROWAVES		INFRARED	
100 m	1 m	1 cm	0.01 cm	1000 nm
Long waves used to send information to TVs, radios, and mobile phones.	Used in microwave ovens, radar, and communication with satellites.		Waves longer than visible red, used for night vision and some telescopes.	

ANSWER THIS

1. Which type of EM wave has the shortest wavelengths?

2. Which EM waves are used for night vision cameras?

3. What's the main difference between mechanical and EM waves?

4. Which waves can cause sunburn?

began to realize there were other electromagnetic waves in the universe. Electromagnetic waves are different from mechanical waves like sound and water waves because they can move through a vacuum, a completely empty space that doesn't even have air in it. You won't find any mechanical waves in outer space, but it's full of electromagnetic waves.

VISIBLE LIGHT Very narrow band of waves that our eyes can see.

ULTRAVIOLET   **X-RAYS**   **GAMMA RAYS**

10 nm   0.01 nm   0.0001 nm

Longer than X-rays but shorter than visible purple, used in many ways but also responsible for sunburn.

Used to produce images of the inside of the body and find things hidden in luggage at airports.

The shortest and most energetic waves, produced by radioactive elements and supernovas.

2.3 VISIBLE LIGHT

Light waves are the fastest-known things in the universe, traveling at about 186,000 miles (300,000 km) per second in a vacuum. If you could move at the speed of light, you'd be able to run around the Earth 7.5 times in a single second.

Light travels in a straight line from its source. When it hits a smooth, shiny surface like a mirror or still water, it is reflected and bounces back off at a single angle, which is why you can see a perfect image of your face in glass. You won't see your face in a carpet or tarmac road; these surfaces are uneven with parts facing all different directions, so light waves bounce off in all directions. This is known as scattering. When light waves pass between two clear substances with different densities (for example, from air to water), they change speed. The change in speed causes refraction, where the light rays bend and change direction—this is why your legs look strange when you stand in a swimming pool.

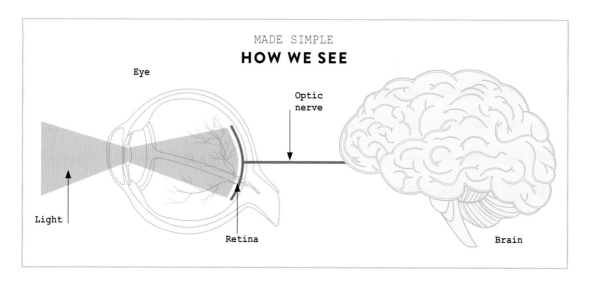

MADE SIMPLE
HOW WE SEE

Eye

Optic nerve

Light

Retina

Brain

FACT Objects can be divided into three groups based on how easily light waves can travel through them. Transparent objects like clear glass let almost all the light waves through, translucent things like tissue paper let some light through, and opaque objects like metal block all light.

REFLECTION

Light reflecting off a smooth surface travels in one direction.

Light reflecting off a rough surface is scattered in different directions.

How we see

When light reflects off a surface, some of the waves travel into our eyes through the pupil. At the back of the eyeball is a tissue called the retina, which is made up of special light-sensitive cells called photoreceptors. These cells send information about the light along a nerve to the brain, and the brain turns this into a picture. When an object stops light waves from traveling any further, no waves reflect off the area behind it. As no light reaches our eyes from this spot, a dark shadow is created.

ANSWER THIS

1. Refraction occurs when light changes _____ and _____.

2. Is a wooden door transparent, translucent, or opaque?

3. What is the name of the light-sensitive tissue in the eye?

4. Which nerve passes information from the eyes to the brain?

REFRACTION

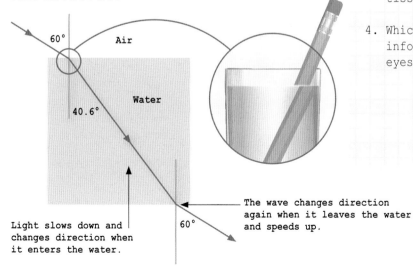

Light slows down and changes direction when it enters the water.

The wave changes direction again when it leaves the water and speeds up.

2.4 COLOR

All the colors around you, from the blue of this book to the yellow of a banana, are created by different wavelengths of light. Humans see colors differently than other animals; it's the brain that decides how each of the wavelengths will look in your mind.

White light is made up of many different colors, each with their own unique frequency. Red has the lowest frequency (longest wavelength), while violet has the highest frequency (shortest wavelength). Between these two colors is a spectrum from long wavelengths to short:
Red > Orange > Yellow > Green > Blue > Indigo > Violet

This is the order of the colors in a rainbow. Tiny water droplets left in the air after rain refract light from the Sun, splitting it into the different colors. Each wavelength slows down inside the water drop and changes direction. Red changes direction the least, while violet slows down and changes the most, so the seven colors end up scattered across the sky. This process is called dispersion.

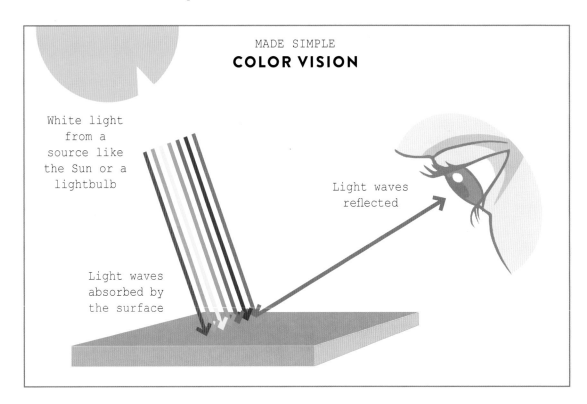

MADE SIMPLE
COLOR VISION

White light from a source like the Sun or a lightbulb

Light waves reflected

Light waves absorbed by the surface

RAINBOW SPECTRUM

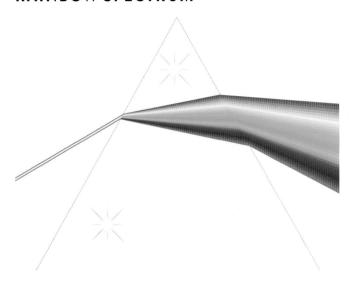

What makes a blue thing blue?

When light waves hit a surface, some are absorbed and the rest bounce back off. The reflected light reaches your eyes, and the brain interprets that as a particular color; if a chair absorbs all of the wavelengths on the spectrum except those that your brain sees as blue, it will look blue. Many objects reflect multiple wavelengths, and the different combinations of light create other shades in your brain like pink and turquoise. If an object reflects all of the light, it will appear white. If it absorbs all the waves then no light is left to be reflected into your eyes, so the object looks black.

ANSWER THIS

1. Which color has the longest wavelength?

2. Which process splits and scatters white light?

3. Which condition makes it hard to tell the difference between colors?

4. If an object absorbs all wavelengths of light it looks _____.

2.5 X-RAYS

If you've ever broken a bone or needed surgery, you will probably have seen the strange image of your own bones. X-rays are the electromagnetic waves that travel through your skin to make these pictures, and they gave the scientist who discovered them a real shock.

X-rays were discovered by accident in 1895 by a German scientist called Wilhelm Röntgen. He named his discovery X-ray because in mathematics "X" means something unknown. While he was investigating the properties of this "new" wave, Röntgen moved his hand in front of the equipment emitting the rays and saw his skeleton appear on a screen. Because X-rays have short wavelengths, they can easily pass through soft tissue like muscle, fat, and skin.

FACT

Historians and archaeologists can use X-rays to look inside objects without breaking them open. Using this method, they've been able to study Egyptian mummies in their stone coffins and discover the 1,000-year-old body of a Buddhist monk hidden inside a statue.

Once news had spread of the amazing new discovery, X-ray machines started to appear at carnivals and fairs as entertainment. In the 1920s, shoe shops began to offer X-rays of children's feet to check there was enough room for their toes in a pair of new shoes. What people didn't realize is that sending too many strong X-rays through the body can be harmful; children trying on lots of pairs of shoes or returning to the shoe shop several times a year could suffer from burned skin and have a higher chance of getting cancer. Since scientists discovered the dangers, X-ray machines have been made much safer and now send fewer waves through the skin.

X-rays today

X-rays are used in hospitals to look at diseases and injuries. Soft parts of the body show up as black or gray because X-rays pass through them, but the waves are blocked by bones so they show up clear and white on the image. This is also how security guards check airport luggage; the pictures on the screen mean they can spot dangerous or illegal items like guns without opening the bags and putting themselves in danger.

AIRPORT X-RAY

X-rays pass through soft items like clothes, but hard objects block the waves and show up as dark shapes on the airport scanner.

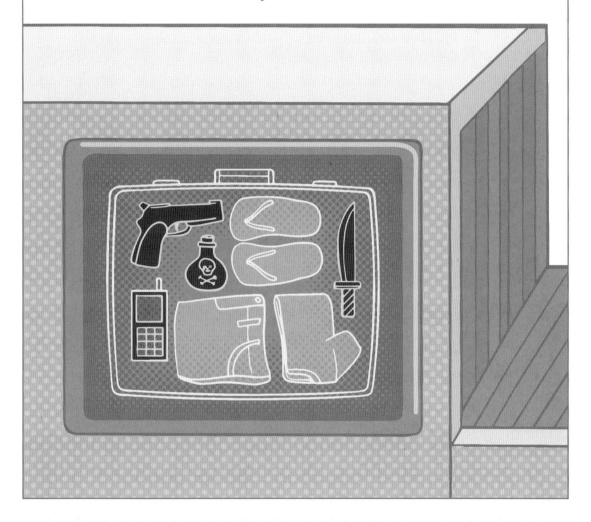

ANSWER THIS

1. When were X-rays discovered?

2. Why was using strong X-rays in shoe shops a bad idea?

3. Which part of the body shows up most clearly on an X-ray?

4. Why are X-rays useful for archaeologists?

2.6 RADIO WAVES

The longest wavelengths on the electromagnetic spectrum belong to radio waves, ranging from 12 inches to several miles. These enormous man-made waves do more than just send music to your radio—they're used for all sorts of tasks from sending emails to watching the weather.

Radio waves are electromagnetic waves that travel by creating vibrations in electrical fields. Messages can be turned into radio waves (like turning words into a secret code), sent through the air, and then "decoded" and turned back into information by electrical equipment like radios, televisions, and computers.

FACT

Radar stands for RAdio Detection And Ranging. It works like echolocation but over much longer distances; radio waves are sent out, and the time it takes for them to reflect and return allows people to work out how far away something is. Radar can be used to keep track of aircraft and ships, and to monitor clouds.

MADE SIMPLE
HD RADIO

Radio stations turn sound into radio waves. The waves are sent to a nearby antenna or radio mast. This transmits the waves and they travel in all directions. When the waves reach radios in homes and cars, they're turned back into sound.

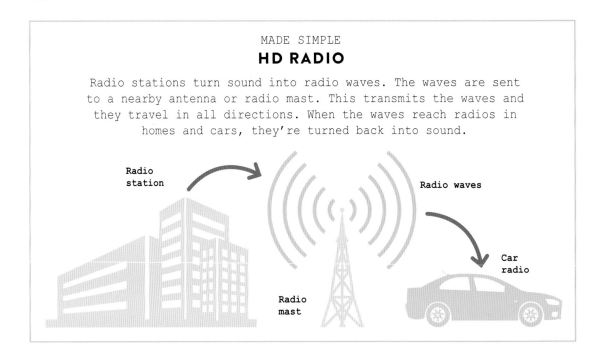

Radio station

Radio waves

Radio mast

Car radio

THE INTERNET

In the past, computers could only access the Internet and communicate with one another if they were connected by cables. Thanks to WiFi, we can connect to the Internet from phones, tablets, and laptops with no cables in sight. Inside modern devices is a component called a wireless adapter, which turns data into radio waves. A box known as a router plugged in somewhere around a house, school, or other building picks up the radio waves, turns them back into data, and sends them along wires called Ethernet connections to the Internet.

Internet

Ethernet cable

Wireless router

Radio waves

Radio waves can travel over long distances because their wavelengths are so long, and they cause no damage if they come into contact with living things, so they're a safe and efficient way of sending information around the world.

Humans have been creating and sending radio waves for more than 100 years, but it wasn't until the 1930s that scientists realized they occur naturally too. Static—the crackling sound that you hear when you move between radio stations—was a mystery until physicist Karl Guthe Jansky worked out that it was caused by natural radio waves traveling to the Earth from space. Since then, astronomers have used radio telescopes that look like giant satellite dishes to study these space signals.

ANSWER THIS

1. Why can radio waves travel over long distances?

2. What causes static on a TV or radio?

3. Which component of a phone or computer turns data into radio waves?

4. What does radar stand for?

2.7 SOUND

Place your hand gently on the front of your throat and hum a line of your favorite song. Can you feel your throat vibrating? All sounds are created by objects vibrating. As they vibrate, they disturb the air around them and send out energy waves.

Sound waves need a medium—a solid, liquid, or gas—that they can move through; if they reach a vacuum or a really thick solid, they won't be able to travel any farther. Sound waves are just like any other wave until they reach a part of a living thing that can process them and turn them into noises. For humans, this is the ear.

INTO THE EAR

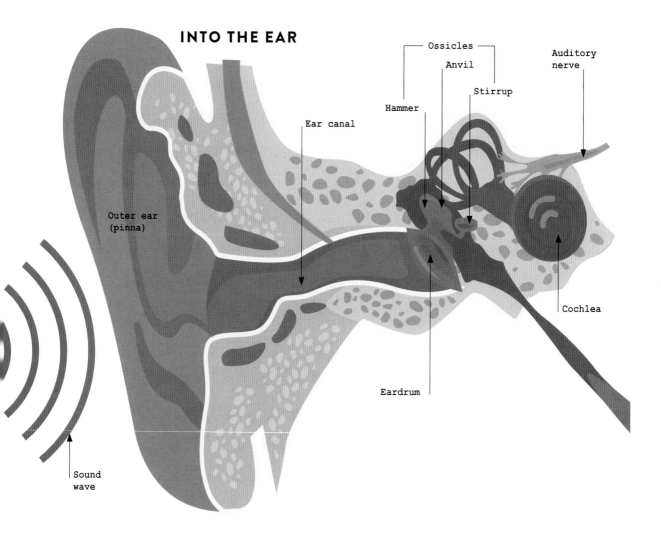

Ossicles

Anvil

Auditory nerve

Stirrup

Hammer

Ear canal

Outer ear (pinna)

Cochlea

Eardrum

Sound wave

How we hear

The outer part of the ear, the pinna, funnels sound waves into the ear canal. At the end of the ear canal is the eardrum, a thin membrane stretched tight, just like a drum. The eardrum vibrates when waves hit it, and these vibrations are passed on to three tiny bones known as the ossicles. The ossicles then transfer the energy to a spiral-shaped sense organ in the inner ear called the cochlea, which turns it into electrical signals and sends them along the auditory nerve to the brain. When the signals arrive, the brain interprets them and turns them into sounds.

The greater the amplitude of a sound wave, the louder the sound will be. Sound waves weaken as they travel, which is why things sound quieter when they're farther away. The speed an object vibrates at changes the pitch of the sound it makes: the faster the vibrations, the higher it will sound. Sound waves can reflect off surfaces like light waves, producing a fainter second sound: an echo.

PITCH

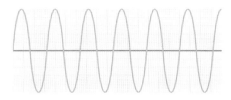

HIGH-PITCHED SOUND
Short wavelength means more waves hit the ear every second; the brain interprets this as a higher pitch.

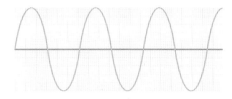

LOW-PITCHED SOUND
Longer wavelength, so fewer waves hit the ear in a second; the brain "hears" this as a low sound.

ANSWER THIS

1. Which part of the ear turns sound waves into electrical signals?

2. What is another name for the outer ear?

3. Which property of a sound wave affects its volume?

4. The shorter the wavelength, the _____ the pitch.

5. What caused the loudest natural sound ever recorded?

2.8 ULTRASOUND AND INFRASOUND

A healthy young person can hear frequencies ranging from 20 to 20,000 hertz. Sound waves with frequencies outside of our hearing range pass by without us ever noticing them, but other animals are communicating with ultrasound and infrasound all around us.

Sounds with frequencies over 20,000 Hz (also written as 20 kHz) are known as ultrasound, because they're too high for humans to hear. Some animals have ears sensitive enough to pick up these waves, including dogs, cats, mice, dolphins, bush babies, and bats.

Bats are famous for their use of ultrasound. They're not completely blind but their vision isn't very good, so they use sound waves to navigate and find food. As a bat flies around it makes ultrasonic clicking noises. When the waves bounce off a surface and return to the bat's ears, its brain works out how much time passed between the click and the returning echo—this tells the bat how far away an object is. Using this technique, known as echolocation, the bat can hunt at high speed without crashing into anything.

FACT

Humans aren't the only ones to be scanned with ultrasound. Vets use the same technology to check inside their animal patients.

Ultrasound scans
Although we can't hear them, humans have found several uses for ultrasound waves. Ships send beams of ultrasound down into the ocean and measure the time it takes for the echo to return to work out how deep the water is. A pregnant woman usually has her tummy scanned with ultrasound so doctors can check that her growing baby is healthy. A piece of equipment called an ultrasonic transducer sends out waves that travel through the skin into the womb and reflect off the baby, and a machine turns the returning echoes into an image.

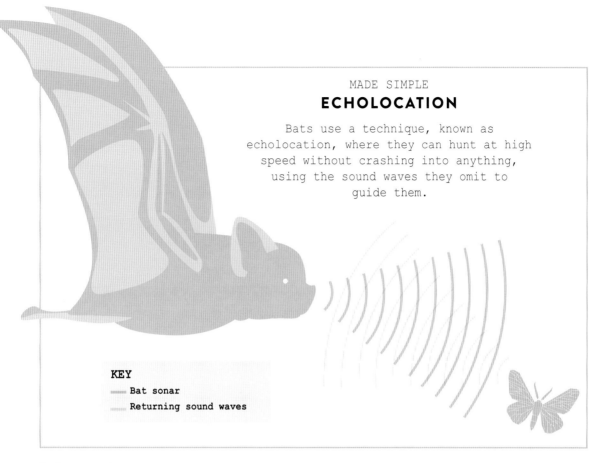

ECHOLOCATION

Bats use a technique, known as echolocation, where they can hunt at high speed without crashing into anything, using the sound waves they omit to guide them.

KEY
— Bat sonar
— Returning sound waves

Infrasound

Sound that travels at frequencies below 20 Hz—infrasound—is too low for humans to hear. Because infrasound waves are so long, they're much better at traveling over distance. Animals like elephants, whales, hippos, and giraffes use infrasound to communicate with other members of their species many miles away.

ANSWER THIS

1. Name two animals that can hear ultrasound.

2. What are bats listening for when they echolocate?

3. Why do doctors scan pregnant women with ultrasound?

4. What can ships measure using ultrasound?

5. Infrasound waves are waves below which frequency?

WAVES

1. **Which of these is not one of the main properties of a wave?**

   a. Amplitude

   b. Frequency

   c. Magnification

   d. Wavelength

2. **How fast does light travel in a vacuum?**

   a. 2,500 miles per hour

   b. 186,000 miles per second

   c. 520,000 miles per minute

   d. 12,000 miles per second

3. **What do bats use to navigate?**

   a. Infrasound

   b. Ultraviolet

   c. Infrared

   d. Ultrasound

4. **What sort of wave is sound?**

   a. Mechanical

   b. Surface

   c. Electromagnetic

   d. Friendly

5. **If an object reflects all wavelengths of light, it looks...**

   a. Red

   b. Black

   c. Violet

   d. White

6. **Which of these can act as a medium for a mechanical wave?**

   a. Outer space

   b. Air

   c. Electrical fields

   d. A vacuum

7. **Which part of an electrical device turns data into radio waves?**

   a. Wireless adapter

   b. Ethernet cable

   c. Internet

   d. Router

8. **How are X-rays used at airports?**

   a. To track planes

   b. To check inside luggage

   c. To send messages

   d. To scan tickets

9. **Which type of EM wave has the longest wavelengths?**

   a. Gamma

   b. Microwave

   c. Radio

   d. X-ray

10. **What is the trough of a wave?**

    a. The lowest point below the rest position

    b. The length of one full wave cycle

    c. The highest point above the rest position

    d. The position of the field or particle when it's not being vibrated

Answers on page 211

SIMPLE SUMMARY

"Wave" describes a disturbance (vibration) that travels through space and matter and transfers energy from one place to another.

- Waves are either mechanical or electromagnetic.

- There are five main properties of waves: amplitude, wavelength, frequency, period, speed.

- Electromagnetic waves are superfast waves that can move without a medium like water or air—they can move through a vacuum.

- Light waves are the fastest-known things in the universe, traveling at about 186,000 miles (300,000 km) per second in a vacuum.

- Humans see colors differently than other animals; it's the brain that decides how each of these wavelengths will look in your mind.

- In X-rays, soft parts of the body show up as black or gray because the waves pass right through them, but the waves are blocked by bones so they show up clear and white on the image.

- Radio waves are electromagnetic waves that travel by creating vibrations in electrical fields.

- The speed an object vibrates at changes the pitch of the sound it makes: the faster the vibrations, the higher it will sound.

- Bats use a technique, known as echolocation, where they can hunt at high speed without crashing into anything using the sound waves they omit to guide them.

3

SPACE

Have you ever looked up at the night sky and wondered what exactly is out there? We can only see a fraction of space; Earth is a tiny speck in an enormous universe full of space rocks, burning balls of gas, and mysterious things we still don't understand.

WHAT YOU WILL LEARN

The universe and the galaxy

Comets, asteroids, and meteors

Stars

The solar system

Earth's orbit

Day and night

The Moon

Humans in space

LESSON
3.1

THE UNIVERSE
AND THE GALAXY

Everything that exists, from our home planet to the distant parts of space we can't see, is part of the universe. Before there was the universe, there was no space, matter, or time. A sudden explosion called the big bang occurred almost 14 billion years ago, producing the energy and matter needed to create the universe.

No one knows how big the universe is, because there's no piece of equipment powerful enough to detect its edge—if it even has an edge—and it's been expanding at high speed ever since the big bang. From observations and mathematical calculations, experts have worked out that the universe is several billion light-years across, but beyond that it's a mystery. A light-year is the distance light can travel across a vacuum in an Earth year: about 5.9 trillion miles (9.5 trillion kilometers). Within the universe are billions of galaxies, each containing millions of stars, planets, and other space objects. Between the galaxies are vast stretches of space containing only dust and a few stray atoms.

THE BIG BANG

Time begins and the universe starts to expand. Particles are formed from the energy. Some of the particles form protons and neutrons. After 380,000 years, temperatures drop enough for atoms to form. Then 300 million years after the big bang, gravity causes clouds of gas to form stars. After another 200 million years, stars start to cluster to become spinning galaxies.

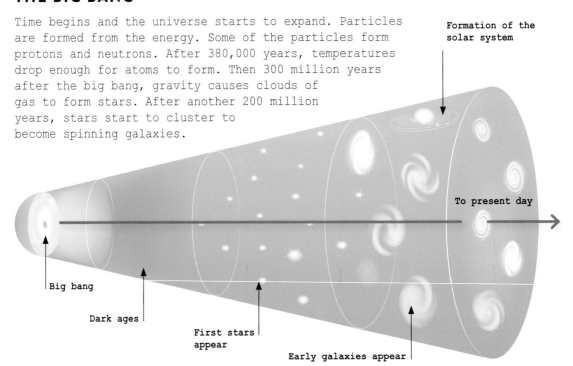

Formation of the solar system

To present day

Big bang

Dark ages

First stars appear

Early galaxies appear

Galaxy groups

Galaxies can be divided into groups based on their shape. These groups include:

- **Elliptical** Stars and other objects grouped together in an oval-shaped disc.
- **Spiral** A galaxy with long "arms" spiraling around the center.
- **Barred spiral** A spiral galaxy with a bar of stars at the center.
- **Irregular** Unusual shapes that don't fit into any of the other groups.

We live in a spiral-shaped galaxy called the Milky Way, which belongs to a collection of about 30 galaxies called the Local Group. There are thought to be around 250 billion stars in the Milky Way. Earth is very small compared to the size of the galaxy—it would take 100,000 light-years to travel from one side of the Milky Way to the other.

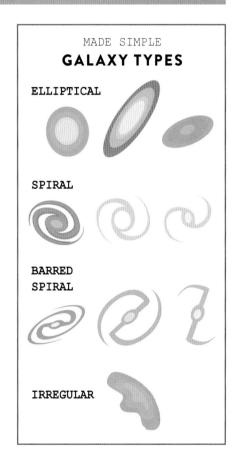

MADE SIMPLE
GALAXY TYPES

ELLIPTICAL

SPIRAL

BARRED SPIRAL

IRREGULAR

ANSWER THIS

1. What type of galaxy is the Milky Way?

2. Which event is believed to have created the universe?

3. When did the first atoms form?

4. How far is it from one side of the Milky Way to the other?

5. How many light-years is 5.9 trillion miles?

LESSON 3.2

COMETS, ASTEROIDS, AND METEORS

When Earth was first forming, space rocks like comets and asteroids played a big part in shaping it and making it the planet it is now. They brought energy and caused the planet to become molten again after it cooled for the first time. It's even thought that water was brought to Earth by a comet.

Individual objects floating around outside of Earth's atmosphere are known as astronomical or celestial bodies. Large bodies are usually classified as planets, but there are smaller objects out there too, including comets, asteroids, and meteoroids.

Comets

A comet is an irregular lump of ice, rock, dirt, and dust moving around the Sun. Comets are usually a few miles across, making them relatively small compared to other space rocks. As an orbiting comet gets close to the Sun, the star's heat melts the ice and turns it into gas. This gas forms a glowing layer called a "coma" around the comet, and mixes with dust to form a long tail streaming out behind it.

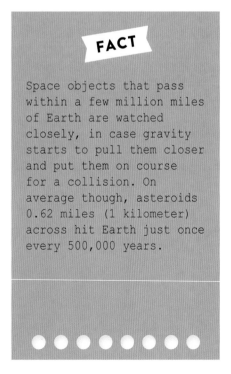

FACT

Space objects that pass within a few million miles of Earth are watched closely, in case gravity starts to pull them closer and put them on course for a collision. On average though, asteroids 0.62 miles (1 kilometer) across hit Earth just once every 500,000 years.

Comets can be divided into two groups based on their journeys around the Sun. Short-period comets take less than 200 years to orbit, while long period comets can have orbits of thousands of years. Halley's Comet, one of the most famous short period comets visible from Earth, comes into view every 75 or 76 years.

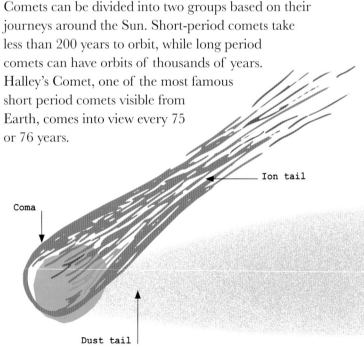

Coma

Ion tail

Dust tail

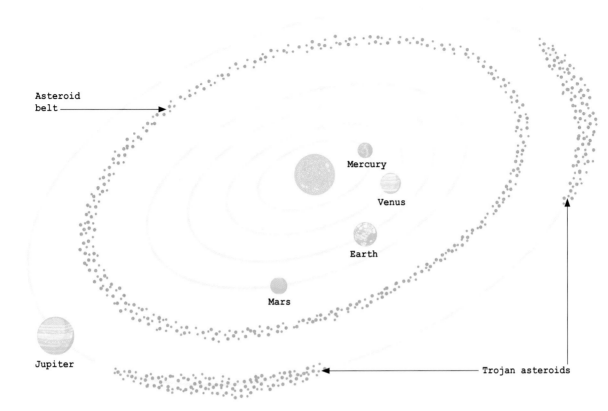

Asteroid belt

Mercury

Venus

Earth

Mars

Jupiter

Trojan asteroids

Asteroids

Asteroids are ancient rock fragments that were created around 4.6 billion years ago when the solar system was formed. Millions orbit the Sun, with most of them moving in a belt between Mars and Jupiter.

Meteors

Meteoroids are small chunks of rock that have broken off from asteroids and comets. Earth's gravity attracts nearby meteoroids and pulls them into its atmosphere, where they're known as meteors. Heat in the atmosphere causes meteors to burn up—the streak of light across the sky as the rock burns is the spectacle we call a shooting star. Some meteors aren't completely destroyed by the heat—when they make it to the ground, they cool into ordinary-looking rocks called meteorites.

ANSWER THIS

1. What is the name for the layer of gas around a warming comet?

2. Short-period comets take less than _____ to orbit the Sun.

3. When does a meteor become a meteorite?

4. Where are most of the solar system's asteroids found?

LESSON
3.3 STARS

On a clear night, the dark sky is lit up by countless twinkling stars. There are at least a billion trillion stars scattered across the universe—that's more than all the grains of sand on Earth. They look delicate and small, but that's just because they're many light-years away.

If you were able to get closer to the stars, you'd see that stars are giant balls of extremely hot gas. The elements helium and hydrogen burn fiercely at the center, sending out heat and light.

FACT

```
Black holes are areas of space with exceptionally
strong gravity. Anything that gets too close is sucked
in and destroyed. Luckily, the nearest black hole to
Earth is 3,000 light-years away.
```

There are many different types of stars, including:

- **Dwarf stars** Relatively small stars that don't burn as brightly as others. Dwarf stars can be different colors, such as red, yellow, white, and brown. Most stars are dwarf stars in the middle years of their lives.
- **Giant stars** Stars often grow and become bright giants as they get older. Some can even turn into supergiants larger than our solar system. Cooler giant stars are red, but the hottest giants glow blue.
- **Neutron stars** Very small stars about 18 miles (30 kilometers) across, made of very tightly packed matter. These dense stars are what's left after a giant star collapses.

Our nearest star is the Sun, a 4.5 billion-year-old yellow dwarf star that we orbit at an average distance of 93 million miles (150 million kilometers). It takes rays of light from the Sun about eight minutes to reach Earth's surface, providing the planet with enough warmth to make life possible. After the Sun, the closest star to Earth is Proxima Centauri, about 4.2 light-years away.

LIFE CYCLE OF A STAR

MAIN SEQUENCE
Stars burn and send out light for billions of years, balanced by gravity.

RED GIANT
When a star begins to run out of fuel, gravity gets weaker and it swells.

PLANETARY NEBULA
The star collapses; outer layers drift away.

WHITE DWARF
The core of the dead star becomes a small and dense clump of matter.

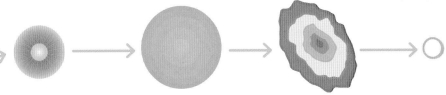

AVERAGE STAR

NEBULA PROTOSTAR
Stars are created from giant clouds of gas and dust. Gravity pulls the matter in the nebula together to form compact clouds called protostars.

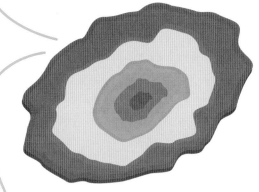

MASSIVE STAR

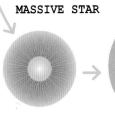

BLACK HOLE
This is created by the collapse of the biggest stars.

MAIN SEQUENCE
Massive stars usually have shorter main sequences than smaller stars.

RED SUPERGIANT
Near the end of its life, a massive star expands.

SUPERNOVA
The core collapses, causing an explosion.

NEUTRON STAR
If the core survives the supernova, it becomes a dense neutron star.

LESSON

3.4 THE SOLAR SYSTEM

Of all the billions of stars in the universe, the Sun is the most important to humans. This dwarf star sits right at the center of the solar system, with eight planets and other space objects orbiting around it.

The Sun makes up more than 99 percent of the mass in the solar system. Its gravity keeps the planets in the solar system on course, stopping them from crashing or moving farther away. The four planets closest to the Sun—including the Earth—are "terrestrial" planets with hard, rocky surfaces. The outer four planets (opposite) are much larger and have surfaces made of swirling gases, giving them the name "gas giants."

THE PLANETS OF THE SOLAR SYSTEM

VENUS
Average distance from Sun: 67 million miles (108 million km)
Features:
- Thick atmosphere
- Acid clouds
- Temperatures remain steady at 864°F (462°C)

MARS
Average distance from Sun: 142 million miles (229 million km)
Features:
- Dust storms
- Deserts   • Two moons
- Temperatures between -225°F (-153°C) and 70°F (20°C)

MERCURY
Average distance from Sun: 35 million miles (56 million km)
Features:
- No atmosphere
- Temperatures between -279°F (-173°C) and 801°F (427°C)

EARTH
Average distance from Sun: 93 million miles (150 million km)
Features:
- Water   • Life   • One moon
- Temperatures between -126°F (-88°C) and 136°F (58°C)

JUPITER
Average distance from Sun: 484 million miles (779 million km)
Features:
- Giant storms
- Gas temperatures of about -234°F (-145°C)
- 79 known moons

NEPTUNE
Average distance from Sun: 2.8 billion miles (4.5 billion km)
Features:
- Thick atmosphere
- 14 moons
- Fastest winds in the solar system
- Average temperature of -353°F (-214°C)

SATURN
Average distance from Sun: 889 million miles (1.5 billion km)
Features:
- Giant rings made of ice, rock, and dust
- Average temperature of -288°F (-178°C)
- 82 known moons

URANUS
Average distance from Sun: 1.8 billion miles (2.9 billion km)
Features:
- Unusual seasons
- 27 moons
- Average cloud temperature of -371°F (-224°C)

ANSWER THIS

1. What sort of planet is Neptune?

2. Which planet is the coldest?

3. Which planet has no atmosphere?

4. How far is Saturn from the Sun?

3.5 EARTH'S ORBIT

The ancient Greeks were confident that the Earth was the center of the solar system and everything else moved around it, but we now know that the Earth moves around the Sun. It's the movement of our planet through space that gives us seasons and birthdays.

Earth's path around the Sun—its orbit—isn't a perfect circle. The shape it makes is more like an oval, described as "elliptical." The Earth moves around the Sun at about 67,000 miles an hour (108,000 km/h)—1,000 times faster than a car on the highway, but this speed isn't always the same. It moves faster through space at the two ends of the oval and slows down slightly as it moves closer to the Sun.

FACT

On a calendar, a year is 365 days long, but Earth actually takes 365 days, 5 hours, 48 minutes, and 45 seconds to complete an orbit. To stop the days of the year getting out of sync with the seasons, there's a leap year every four years.

MADE SIMPLE
THE EARLY SOLAR SYSTEM

Ancient scientists incorrectly placed Earth at the center of the solar system, this was known as the geocentric model. The correct model, with the planets orbiting the Sun, is called the heliocentric model.

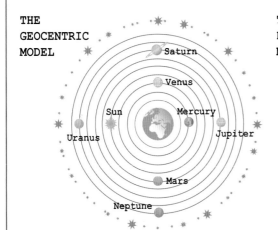

THE GEOCENTRIC MODEL

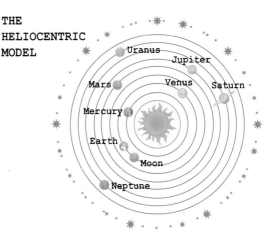

THE HELIOCENTRIC MODEL

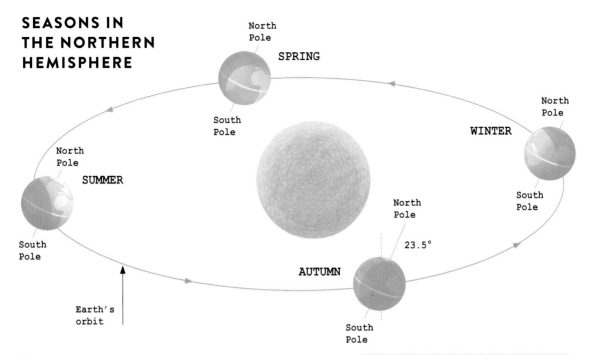

SEASONS IN THE NORTHERN HEMISPHERE

North Pole

SPRING

South Pole

North Pole

WINTER

SUMMER

North Pole

South Pole

South Pole

North Pole

23.5°

AUTUMN

Earth's orbit

South Pole

Years

Even though it moves at thousands of miles an hour, it takes Earth 365 days to complete one loop around the Sun: one Earth year. Every birthday, the planet is at the same point in the orbit as the day you were born. A year is a different length of time on the other planets in the solar system, because they move at different speeds and have different distances to travel to complete a circuit. Mercury, the closest planet to the Sun, takes just 87 days, but a year on Jupiter is the same as 12 Earth years.

Seasons

Earth spins on its axis, but the axis isn't in line with its orbit. This means that rather than spinning like a top or rolling around the Sun like a wheel, Earth is tilted at an angle of 23.5°. When part of the world is tilted away from the Sun, it receives less heat energy and goes through winter. At the same time, the other side of the world is closer to the Sun and gets hotter weather. Places closer to the poles experience more extreme seasons, while areas around the Equator stay a more constant distance from the Sun.

3.6 DAY AND NIGHT

Earth spins as it orbits the Sun. A day is the amount of time it takes to complete one turn, and on Earth a day is 24 hours long. As well as having different year lengths, other planets have different day lengths too—a single rotation of Venus takes 5,832 hours.

To us, it looks like the Sun rises every morning, moves across the sky, and then goes back down at night. Ancient civilizations believed that gods pulled the Sun through the sky each day. The Sun is actually staying still, and we're the ones moving. The Earth spins from west to east, so it appears that the Sun rises in the east and sets in the west.

DAY AND NIGHT

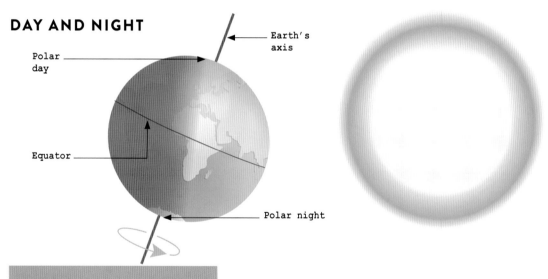

Earth's axis

Polar day

Equator

Polar night

FACT

The tilt of the Earth causes the poles to each have six months of constant light and six months of constant darkness. Without a watch it's impossible to know what time it is at the poles.

The Sun can only shine on half of the Earth at once. The side facing it receives heat and light, while the side facing out into space is in shadow—this is what causes day and night. As the Earth spins, different parts of the planet face the Sun, so night and day happen at different times depending on the country you're in. The globe is divided up into 24 "time zones" so that the time matches up with day and night all around the world. When it's 12 noon in London, it's only 7 a.m. in New York. Some countries, like America and Russia, are so big that they cover several time zones.

Days and seasons

Unless you live on the equator, you'll notice that day and night change length throughout the year; days are long in summer, but it gets dark much earlier in winter. The Sun also appears to take a different path through the sky, climbing higher in the summer. This is because of the Earth's tilt. During summer, you're tilted toward the Sun, so it's visible in the sky for longer, but in winter, you're tilted away.

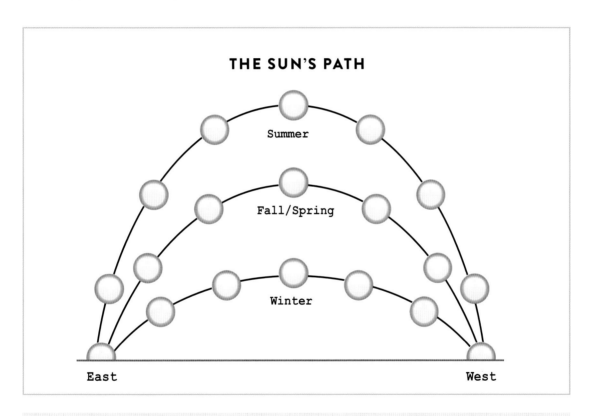

THE SUN'S PATH

Summer

Fall/Spring

Winter

East   West

ANSWER THIS

1. Which way does the Earth spin?

2. Which season has the longest days?

3. How many time zones are there?

4. Which parts of the world are in darkness for half the year?

3.7 THE MOON

Scientists think that the Moon was formed when a lump of molten rock was knocked off a very young Earth. Rather than drifting off into space, it was held by Earth's gravity and began to orbit as a satellite—an object that moves around a planet.

The Moon is a lump of rock about a quarter of the size of Earth. It doesn't emit its own light, but we can see it because it reflects light from the Sun. The Moon turns as it orbits, completing a rotation every 27 days, so we always see the same side—the part facing away from us is the "dark side."

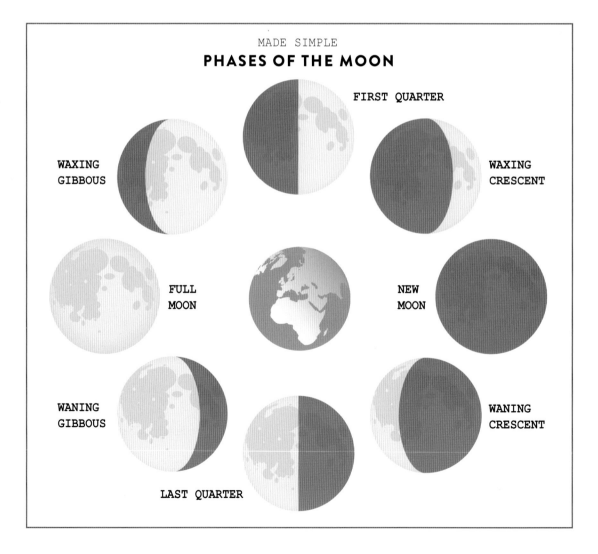

MADE SIMPLE
PHASES OF THE MOON

FIRST QUARTER

WAXING GIBBOUS

WAXING CRESCENT

FULL MOON

NEW MOON

WANING GIBBOUS

WANING CRESCENT

LAST QUARTER

SPRING TIDE

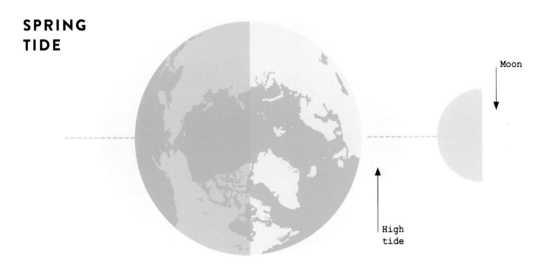

Moon

High tide

The Moon seems to change shape each night because when the Earth is in between the Moon and Sun it casts a shadow, so only part of the Moon can be lit up. The Moon goes through eight different shapes, known as "phases." The time it takes for the Moon to go through all eight phases is known as a lunar month, or synodic month. The months of the calendar can be 28, 29, 30, or 31 days long, but a lunar month always lasts 29.5 days. The Moon takes just over 27 days to complete an orbit of the Earth (a sidereal month), but because the Earth is turning and moving around the Sun at the same time, it takes a bit longer for us to see all eight phases.

Tides

The Moon's gravitational force attracts the water on the side of the Earth closest to it, causing it to bulge out toward space. This is known as tidal force, creating high tides. As that part of the Earth spins away from the Moon, the pull of gravity weakens and the water goes back down, causing a low tide.

ANSWER THIS

1. Why can we see the Moon?

2. When part of the world is facing the Moon, which tide does it experience?

3. How many phases does the Moon go through?

4. Why don't we see the dark side of the Moon?

HUMANS IN SPACE

People have gazed up at the sky for 2 million years, but the first human ventured into outer space less than a hundred years ago. Now, just a few decades later, attention is turning to our nearest neighboring planet.

In 1961, a Russian cosmonaut called Yuri Gagarin became the first human in outer space when he was launched through the atmosphere in a rocket and his capsule completed an orbit of Earth. The United States and the Soviet Union (a state that included countries like Russia, Georgia, and Ukraine) had been competing with each other for years to be the first to send a person into space. This was known as the Space Race, and Gagarin secured a victory for the Soviet Union.

The Space Race didn't end with Gagarin's journey; next, the competitors set their sights on the Moon. In 1969, the Apollo 11 Lunar Module Eagle touched down and astronauts Neil Armstrong and Buzz Aldrin became the first people to walk on the Moon.

HOW A ROCKET WORKS

Newton's Third Law of Motion states that every action has an equal and opposite reaction. Gases are pushed down from the rocket's engine at high speed, and the rocket is lifted into the sky with equal force.

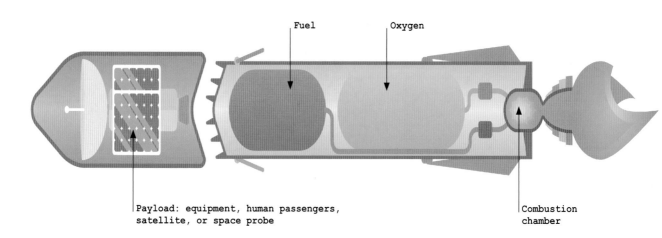

Fuel

Oxygen

Payload: equipment, human passengers, satellite, or space probe

Combustion chamber

A SPACESUIT

Spacesuits are packed with everything an astronaut needs to stay safe and comfortable while they carry out tasks.

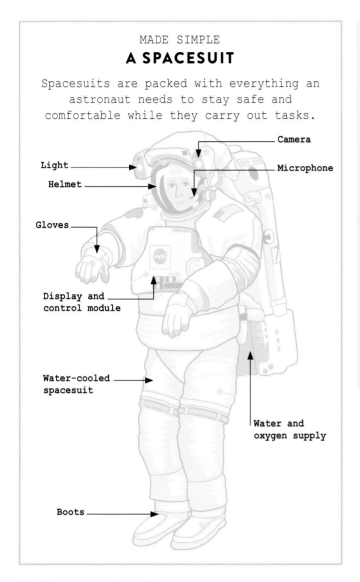

- Camera
- Microphone
- Light
- Helmet
- Gloves
- Display and control module
- Water-cooled spacesuit
- Water and oxygen supply
- Boots

Modern space travel

Since Yuri Gagarin's orbit, over 500 people have been into space. In 1998 space agencies from five countries worked together to launch the International Space Station (ISS), the length of a football field that orbits Earth 15.5 times a day. Over 200 people from 19 different countries have visited the ISS, with some staying for almost a year.

Space agencies are becoming more and more ambitious. Unmanned devices have already landed on Mars and sent back information about the planet. Now, plans are being made for astronauts to make the journey, and some people hope we might even be able to settle there!

SPACE

1. A light-year is...

a. The distance light travels in air in a year

b. The amount of light that reaches Earth in a year

c. The distance light travels in a vacuum in a year

d. A year with one extra day

2. What type of star is the Sun?

a. White dwarf

b. Red giant

c. Neutron star

d. Yellow dwarf

3. Why do we have seasons?

a. Because the Sun sometimes shines brighter

b. Because Earth is tilted

c. Because the Moon blocks the Sun

d. Because of the Earth's spin

4. What is a meteor called when it lands on Earth?

a. Meteoroid

b. Asteroid

c. Comet

d. Meteorite

5. Which of these has the most impact on the tides?

a. The gravitational pull of the Moon

b. The spin of the Earth

c. The gravitational pull of the Sun

d. The Earth's orbit

6. Where does the Sun rise?

a. In the north

b. In the south

c. In the east

d. In the west

7. When did the first humans land on the Moon?

a. 1969

b. 1912

c. 2004

d. 1998

8. How old is the universe?

a. Almost 16 million years

b. Almost 14 billion years

c. Almost 18 trillion years

d. Almost 19 million years

9. Which planet has distinctive rings?

a. Saturn

b. Venus

c. Mercury

d. Mars

10. How many phases does the Moon go through?

a. 10

b. 6

c. 12

d. 8

Answers on page 212

SIMPLE SUMMARY

Everything that exists, from our home planet to the distant parts of space we can't see, is part of the universe.

- The universe has been expanding at high speed ever since the big bang.

- Within the universe are billions of galaxies, each containing millions of stars, planets, and other space objects.

- We live in a spiral-shaped galaxy called the Milky Way, which belongs to a collection of over 30 galaxies called the Local Group.

- Planets, comets, asteroids, and meteoroids float around outside of Earth's atmosphere.

- There are at least a billion trillion stars scattered across the universe—that's more than all the grains of sand on Earth.

- The Sun is the most important star to humans, and sits at the center of the solar system, with eight planets and other space objects orbiting around it.

- Even though it moves at thousands of miles an hour, it takes Earth 365 days to complete one loop around the Sun: one Earth year.

- As the Earth spins, different parts of the planet face the Sun.

- The Moon goes through eight different phases—the time it takes to do this is known as a lunar month.

- In 1961, Yuri Gagarin became the first human in outer space.

- The International Space Station (ISS) is the length of a football field that orbits Earth 15.5 times a day.

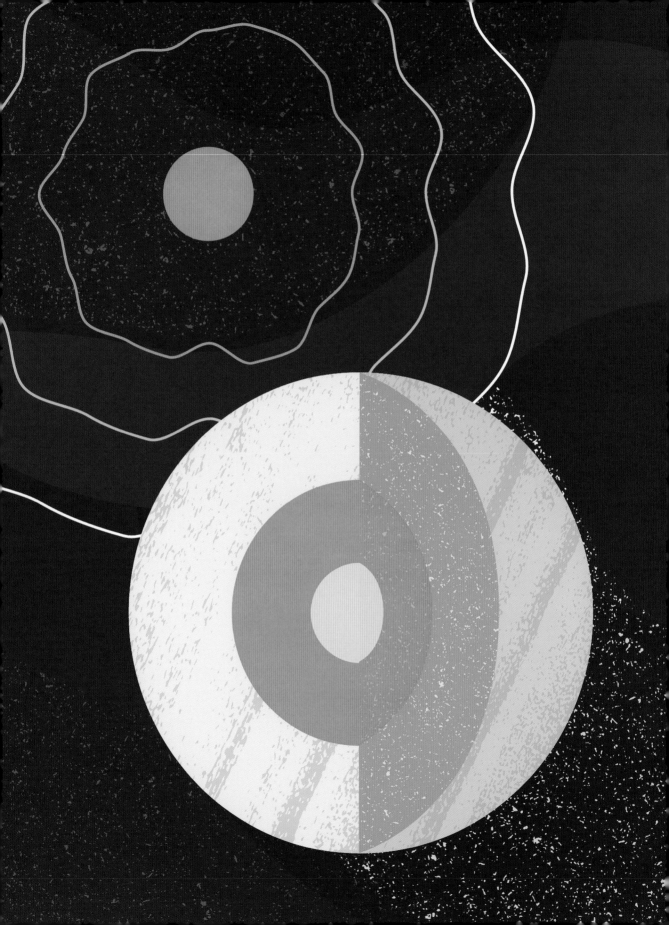

4
EARTH SCIENCES

Mountains, cliffs, rocks, and lakes look like they have been standing still since time began, but our planet is always shifting and changing. Take a peek under the Earth's surface to discover how rocks are formed, why volcanoes erupt, and why the continents aren't where they used to be.

WHAT YOU WILL LEARN

Formation of the Earth

Earth's atmosphere

Tectonics

Volcanoes and earthquakes

Rocks and minerals

Weathering

The water cycle

Weather and climate

FORMATION OF THE EARTH

Once there was only empty space where Earth is now. It took billions of years and a remarkable series of events to create the planet we call home.

The story of our planet began more than 4.6 billion years ago. At that time, clouds of gas and dust had formed all across the universe. These giant clouds were made of the elements hydrogen and helium, created in the big bang (see page 50), and heavier elements made in the centers of the first stars. Within each cloud, gravity pulled these materials together. Nudged by a supernova—the explosion of a nearby dying star—the cloud, or "nebula," that would one day be our solar system became a spinning disk with a star at its center, and the floating particles started to clump together into planets.

FACT When Earth was still a young planet and had not yet begun to cool, a large object, possibly another planet, bumped into it. The impact of the crash knocked off some of the molten rock, which drifted into orbit around our planet and became the Moon.

MADE SIMPLE
THE FORMATION OF EARTH

4.6 BILLION YEARS AGO
Particles collect in bands around a star.

4.6–4.2 BILLION YEARS AGO
Gas and molten matter combine to form planets, including Earth.

4.1 BILLION YEARS AGO
Denser material gathers in the center.

3.8 BILLION YEARS AGO
Earth's surface cools and a rocky crust is formed.

EARTH'S LAYERS

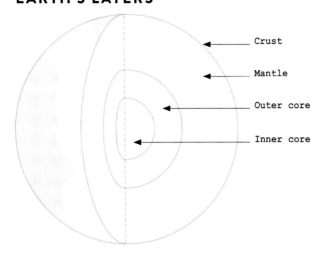

- Crust
- Mantle
- Outer core
- Inner core

CRUST
3–40 miles (5–64 km) thick
MANTLE
1,775 miles (2,855 km) thick
OUTER CORE
1,240 miles (2,000 km) thick
INNER CORE
1,520 miles (2,450 km) in diameter

Becoming Earth

As Earth grew, so did its gravitational pull, and for 500 million years the planet was pelted with lumps of matter that kept it hot and molten (melted). The planet attracted gases, forming the atmosphere, and the surface cooled to form a crust. This first cooling happened about 4.1 billion years ago, but a second wave of meteoroids, asteroids, and comets turned it all back to liquid. When the space showers finally stopped about 3.8 billion years ago, the crust solidified for a second time.

Earth's layers

The very middle of the Earth—the inner core—is a ball of metal (mostly iron and nickel) measuring about 1,520 miles (2,450 kilometers) across. The core is so hot that usually the metals would melt, but the pressure from the layers above squashes it and keeps it solid. The outer core is a layer of molten metal wrapped around the inner core. Floating on this liquid is the mantle, a thick layer of partly molten rock that makes up over 80 percent of the planet's volume. The crust is the hard layer on the Earth's surface, wrapping everything up like the pastry in a pie.

> **ANSWER THIS**
>
> 1. When did Earth start to cool for a second time?
>
> 2. How thick is the outer core?
>
> 3. What was formed after a space object crashed into Earth?
>
> 4. Which metals make up most of the inner core?
>
> 5. Which is the thickest of Earth's layers?

LESSON 4.2 EARTH'S ATMOSPHERE

All around the Earth are layers of gases that together make up the planet's atmosphere. Not only do these invisible layers provide us with air to breathe, they also protect us from objects flying through space and the full force of the Sun.

The atmosphere is made up of a combination of gases, plus other substances like dust and volcanic smoke that have risen up from the Earth. Nitrogen gas makes up 78 percent of the atmosphere, 21 percent is oxygen, 1 percent is argon, and 0.04 percent is carbon dioxide. The rest is made up of small amounts of other gases like helium, methane, and neon.

There are five main layers in the atmosphere. From the ground up, these are the troposphere, the stratosphere, the mesosphere, the thermosphere, and the exosphere. The exosphere—the outer layer—has no real outer edge; gases here get thinner and thinner until they blend into space.

The ozone layer
The ozone layer is a part of the stratosphere that contains a much higher concentration of ozone gas than the rest of the atmosphere. This gas absorbs lots of the Sun's harmful ultraviolet (UV) rays and stops them from reaching Earth; UV rays cause sunburn and damage eyes, so the ozone layer is crucial for our health and survival.

ANSWER THIS

1. How many layers make up the atmosphere?

2. Which layer is the farthest away from us?

3. What does the ozone layer protect us from?

4. What percentage of the atmosphere is nitrogen?

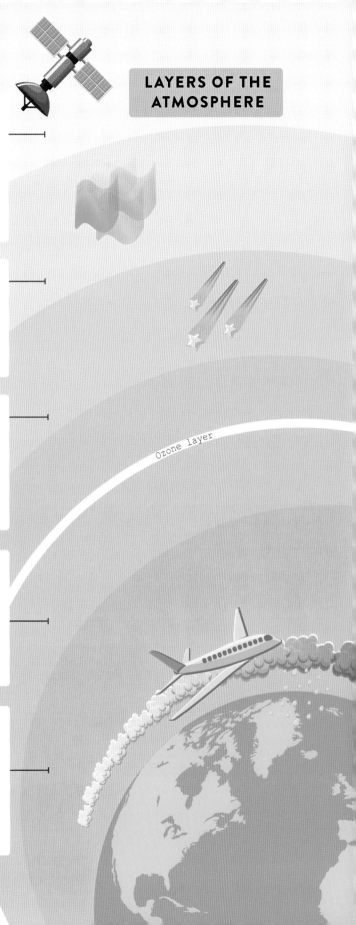

EXOSPHERE

The outermost layer of the atmosphere lies 500 miles (800 km) above the Earth's surface. The air is thin. Gas molecules drift in as there is no boundary between the exosphere and outer space.

THERMOSPHERE

The top of the thermosphere is 400 miles (640 km) away. Temperatures are high as air molecules absorb the Sun's radiation.

MESOSPHERE

The top of the mesosphere is 50 miles (80 km) above us. Temperatures decrease down to -148°F (-100°C) at the top. Meteors usually burn up here.

Ozone layer

STRATOSPHERE

The stratosphere starts 6-12 miles (10-20 km) above Earth and ends 31 miles (50 km) away. Temperatures vary from -76°F (-60°C) to just above freezing.

TROPOSPHERE

The troposphere is about 12 miles (20 km) high at the equator and 6 miles (10 km) high at the poles. It contains 80 percent of the gas in the atmosphere. All weather happens in this "weather layer."

LESSON 4.3 TECTONICS

As solid as it may feel, the Earth's crust is always on the move. Pieces called tectonic plates float around very slowly on the mantle, creating mountains, earthquakes, and volcanoes as they move apart and bump into one other.

As we've seen, the inner core of the Earth is extremely hot. Heat rises, and some of the heat travels through the outer core and reaches the mantle. As molten rock at the bottom of the mantle is heated, it moves toward the surface and spreads out under the crust before cooling and sinking back down again. This movement creates circles of moving rock called convection currents. The currents make the fragments of crust balanced on the mantle move around like boats drifting on the sea. All of this happens very slowly—on average, plates move at about the same speed as your fingernails grow.

FACT

All of the land on Earth used to be joined together in a single mass. This "supercontinent" called Pangaea broke apart about 175 million years ago, and the pieces drifted away from one other to form the continents we know today.

TECTONIC PLATES

No one is really sure how many plates there are. Here are some of the biggest ones, with the directions they're moving in at the moment.

KEY

— Plate boundary

→ Plate movement

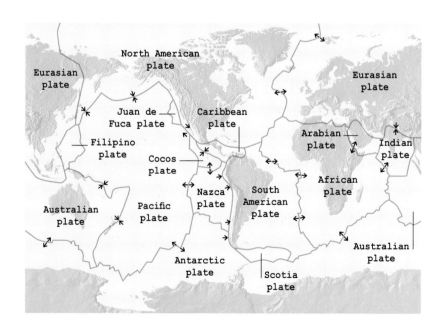

North American plate
Eurasian plate
Eurasian plate
Juan de Fuca plate
Caribbean plate
Arabian plate
Indian plate
Filipino plate
Cocos plate
African plate
Nazca plate
South American plate
Australian plate
Pacific plate
Australian plate
Antarctic plate
Scotia plate

EARTH'S BOUNDARIES

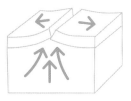
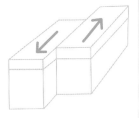

DESTRUCTIVE PLATE BOUNDARY
As the plates converge, the heavier oceanic plate is pushed under the continental plate and into the mantle. The oceanic plate melts, and the molten rock can erupt.

COLLISION ZONE
When two continental plates collide, neither is forced down because neither one is heavier. They push each other upward, forming "fold mountains," like the Alps and the Himalayas.

CONSTRUCTIVE BOUNDARY
Also known as a divergent boundary, this boundary is found where plates move apart. Molten rock called magma rises from the mantle to fill the gap, then cools to form new crust.

CONSERVATIVE BOUNDARY
Also known as a transformational boundary, plates here move past one another in opposite directions and crust is neither created nor destroyed. Friction can build up and set off earthquakes.

There are two main types of tectonic plates:
- **Oceanic** Heavy plates found under the bottom of the world's oceans.
- **Continental** Thicker than oceanic plates but not as heavy; the very thickest parts rise above the sea as land. The seven major continental plates make up Earth's seven continents.

At the boundaries
The edges of tectonic plates are known as boundaries. Where plates meet or move apart, crust can either be destroyed or created. As you'll find out, earthquakes and volcanoes are much more likely to be found at plate boundaries (see page 76).

ANSWER THIS

1. What moves the tectonic plates?

2. What are the names of the two types of plate?

3. Which plate boundary creates new crust?

4. Which type of plate is heaviest?

5. How long ago did Pangaea break apart?

LESSON 4.4 VOLCANOES AND EARTHQUAKES

Shooting burning material up to 28 miles (45 km) into the air and shaking the ground so hard that buildings collapse, volcanoes and earthquakes are among the most impressive—and dangerous— displays of the power hidden within our planet.

Volcanoes are openings in the Earth's crust. Many are found in mountains, with long tubes called shafts running down from the peak toward the mantle. Most volcanoes spring up at plate boundaries, but they can also form away from the edges over plumes of especially hot rock. When a volcano erupts, magma, gas, and ash burst out from deep inside the Earth. Magma is called lava once it leaves the volcano and flows out from the crater. Volcanoes are described as active, dormant, or extinct.

INSIDE A VOLCANO

MAGMA CHAMBER: Underground pool of molten rock
MAIN VENT: Opening running into the Earth
CRATER: Bowl-shaped dip created by a volcano's first eruption
SECONDARY VENT: Lava can erupt from other spots on the volcano
VOLCANIC BOMBS: Lumps of rock and other material
PLUME: Cloud of ash, steam, and volcanic gas
LAHAR: Mudslide set off when lava and ash mix with mud and water on the volcano's slope
LAVA: Magma above the surface, reaches up to 2,282°F (1,250°C)

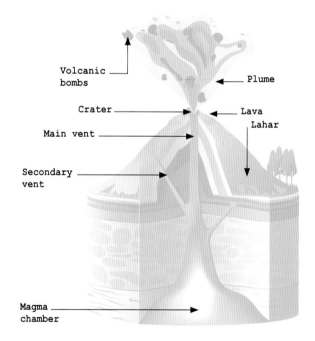

 FACT Most of the world's volcanoes and earthquakes are found in an area of the world called the Ring of Fire that runs in an arc around the edge of the Pacific Ocean. Oceanic crust is being pushed under continental crust all around the arc, causing frequent tremors and eruptions.

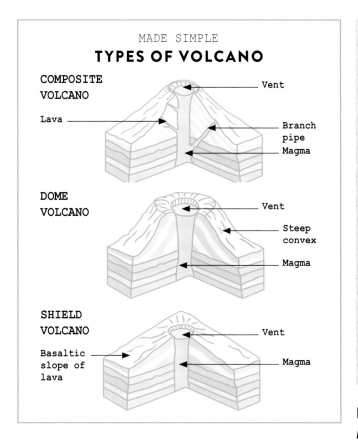

MADE SIMPLE
TYPES OF VOLCANO

COMPOSITE VOLCANO — Vent

Lava — Branch pipe — Magma

DOME VOLCANO — Vent — Steep convex — Magma

SHIELD VOLCANO — Vent — Basaltic slope of lava — Magma

ANSWER THIS

1. What temperature can lava reach?

2. Which scale is used to measure the strength of an earthquake?

3. Would you feel a Magnitude 1.8 earthquake?

4. What is created when lava and ash combine with water and mud?

5. Where are most of the world's volcanoes found?

EARTHQUAKE MAGNITUDE

Minor	**2.5 OR LESS:** Usually not felt, recorded by seismometer
Light	**2.5-5.4:** Felt but causes little damage
Moderate	**5.5-6.0:** Minor damage to buildings
Strong	**6.1-6.9:** Serious damage in built-up areas
Major	**7.0-7.9:** Severe ground shaking, causes major damage
Great	**8.0 AND ABOVE:** Can destroy whole cities

Earthquakes

Tectonic plates move past one another at conservative boundaries, but they don't always move smoothly—sometimes they get stuck. Convection currents keep pushing the plates until suddenly they start moving again with a jolt. The release of built-up energy can trigger an earthquake, a series of shock waves rippling through the surrounding rock from the epicenter (the point where the plates jolted).

Hundreds of earthquakes happen around the world every day, but most are so small no one notices them. Their strength is measured on the Moment Magnitude Scale—every step up the scale means the shock waves are 10 times bigger than the level below. Earthquakes above a six on the scale can shake the ground so much that houses collapse and cracks appear in the crust.

LESSON
4.5

ROCKS AND MINERALS

The Pyramids, the Easter Island statues, and Stonehenge—all of these impressive creations were carved and built hundreds of years ago. They've lasted so long because they are made of rock, the hard material that forms most of our planet.

Rocks are formed from combinations of minerals, which are natural solid substances made of one or more element. There are three main types of rocks, grouped by how they came to exist.

Obsidian is a dark igneous rock, so smooth and shiny that it's sometimes called "natural glass." It's formed when lava cools so quickly that there is only time for tiny crystals to form. Cut obsidian is very sharp, and Stone Age hunters used it to make spearheads and arrowheads.

Soil is made from a mixture of tiny rock pieces, plant and animal remains, water, and air. The amount of each "ingredient" in an area's soil determines the types of plant that grow well there.

Igneous rock

When magma (molten rock) cools, it forms igneous rock. This can happen as magma cools beneath the Earth's surface, or when lava cools after a volcanic explosion. Intrusive rock—igneous rock made inside the Earth—is formed slowly and contains large crystals, whereas extrusive rock—rock made from lava—forms quickly and has small crystals. Most igneous rock is incredibly hard; this group includes granite, which is used to make tiles, bridges, and even whole buildings.

Sedimentary rock

As rocks are broken and worn down, small pieces known as sediment end up in rivers and get carried along by the water. When the river reaches an ocean, the current slows down and the pieces of rock fall to the bottom. Over millions of years, lots of sediment is deposited in the same place, and the weight of it all squashes (or compacts) the pieces at the bottom. Layers of rock build up, often different in color because the type of sediment being deposited changes over time—some layers even have fossils hidden among the rock pieces (see page 186).

Metamorphic rock

Metamorphosis is the process of one thing turning into another, like a caterpillar turning into a butterfly, and metamorphic rocks such as marble and slate are formed when existing rock is changed by heat and pressure.

THE ROCK CYCLE

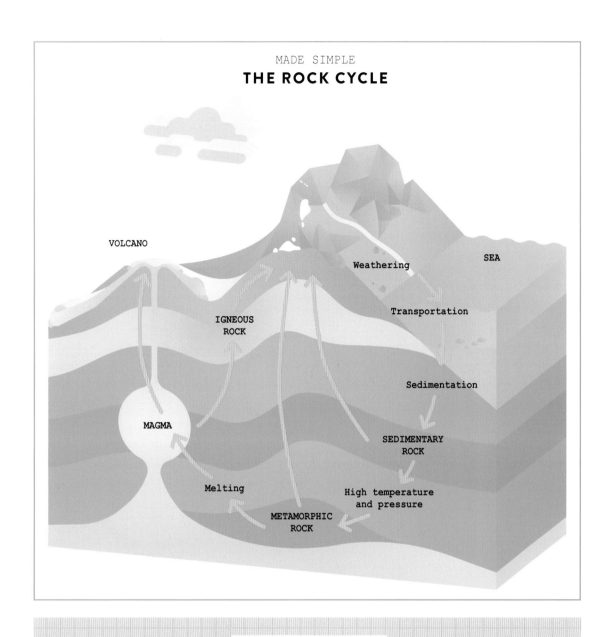

VOLCANO

SEA

Weathering

Transportation

IGNEOUS
ROCK

Sedimentation

MAGMA

SEDIMENTARY
ROCK

Melting

High temperature
and pressure

METAMORPHIC
ROCK

ANSWER THIS

1. Which type of rock is formed in layers?

2. Which cools faster, intrusive or extrusive igneous rock?

3. What are all rocks made of?

4. Which rock is known as "natural glass"?

5. What is the name for the pieces of rock that settle on the seabed?

LESSON
4.6 WEATHERING

Rocks are tough, but they're not invincible. Every day, plants, chemicals, and weather wear away at them—over a long time this can cause them to crack or break.

Rocks are broken, destroyed, and changed when tectonic plates meet (see page 75), but this isn't weathering. Weathering is when rocks are gradually broken down or worn away where they are. There are three main types of weathering: biological, chemical, and physical.

FACT After weathering has broken or worn a rock into smaller and smaller pieces, wind, water, and ice carry some of them away to new places. This is called erosion, and it's the process that creates cliffs and valleys.

Biological weathering
Animals and plants can weather rocks. Plants in rocky areas send their roots deep into any cracks they find—as the plants grow and the roots get thicker, the two sides are pushed farther apart and the rock can split. Animals (including humans) wear rocks down as they walk, hop, or run over them, and some burrowing animals scrape away at holes and cracks to make their homes.

Chemical weathering

Carbon dioxide in the air dissolves into rainwater and makes it slightly acidic, which can cause the rain to react with the minerals that make up the rock. Rocks like granite can mostly withstand the effects of rain, but "soft" rocks like chalk and limestone are easily weathered by it. Burning fossil fuels release carbon dioxide and another gas called sulfur dioxide into the atmosphere. When sulfur dioxide dissolves in clouds, it makes the rain more acidic than usual. This acid rain "eats" at old buildings and statues, especially those made from softer rocks.

Physical weathering

Physical processes such as changes in temperature and the force of rain, wind, and waves can weather rocks. Rocks expand ever so slightly when they're hot and shrink a little when they're cold. If this expanding and contracting happens many times it can lead to cracking—this happens in places like the desert where it's scorching in the day and freezing at night. In addition, the wind can blow grains of sand and dust against rock, and heavy rain and crashing waves wear away at it. If water gets into the cracks and freezes, the expansion caused by the formation of ice crystals pushes the rock and makes the cracks even bigger— this is called freeze-thaw.

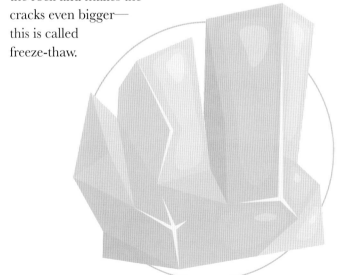

> **ANSWER THIS**

1. Which type of rock is damaged most by chemical weathering?

2. Which part of a plant can crack rock?

3. What is the name of the gas that creates acid rain?

4. What happens to rocks when they warm up?

5. Which process moves weathered rock to new places?

4.7 THE WATER CYCLE

The hydrosphere is the name for all the water on the planet. Earth's water has been moving around for more than 4 billion years, so when you drink a glass of water you're drinking water that has been drunk by dinosaurs, sailed on by Viking ships, and held in the sky as a cloud.

Water is constantly moving around the globe and being recycled in a process known as the water or hydrologic cycle ("hydro" comes from the Greek word for water). As water moves between the land, the sea, and the sky, it can also change from solid to liquid to gas and back again.

THE WATER CYCLE

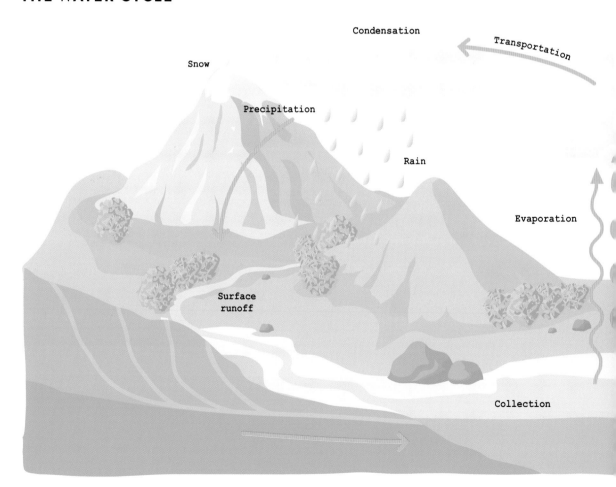

FACT Water that lands on soil and leaves is absorbed and used by plants. On warm days, plants open the tiny holes on the underneath of their leaves. Some of the water inside the leaves turns to vapor and escapes through the holes into the air in a process known as transpiration.

Evaporation

When the Sun's rays hit lakes, rivers, ponds, and oceans they heat the water at the surface. This water turns into a gas called water vapor, which rises up into the air.

Condensation

As the vapor reaches cooler air higher up in the atmosphere, it condenses, turning back into little drops of liquid water. Millions of tiny droplets group together and form clouds suspended in the air. Wind and air currents transport the clouds around the sky.

Precipitation

Eventually, so many drops join together that the cloud becomes heavy. Once the air can no longer hold the cloud up, water drops fall to the earth. When the air is very cold, the water falls as sleet, hail, or snow, but in warmer air it becomes rain. "Precipitation" is the name for any type of falling water.

Collection

Some precipitation falls straight into bodies of water like streams and oceans. Melting snow and heavy rain become "surface runoff," water that flows over land until it either reaches a body of water or soaks into the ground. Wherever it falls, water will one day evaporate and start the cycle again.

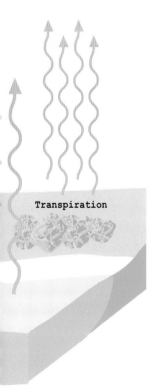

Transpiration

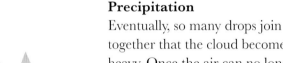

> **ANSWER THIS**
>
> 1. What is precipitation?
>
> 2. How long has water been moving around the planet?
>
> 3. What is the name for water in its gaseous phase?
>
> 4. What causes evaporation?
>
> 5. What is the other name for the water cycle?

WEATHER AND CLIMATE

LESSON
4.8

Weather is the set of conditions you can see when you look out of the window. It determines whether you need sunglasses or an umbrella, and whether you wear a T-shirt or a woolly sweater. Climate, on the other hand, is the average set of weather conditions over a long period of time.

Lots of things affect weather conditions and climate. Places near the equator—the imaginary line around the Earth, halfway between the North and South Poles—are closer to the Sun, so they experience more hot and sunny days. The height of a place is an important factor too—high places like mountains are often cold with lots of snow. Currents in the air can bring warm or cold air from other areas, and the wind pushes clouds around the sky. The sea heats up and cools down more slowly than the land, so places by the coast are kept warm in the winter.

FACT

Air rises when heat from the Sun warms it. As the warm air moves up, cold air rushes in from somewhere else to fill the gap it leaves behind. This fast movement of air creates gusts of wind.

Clouds can look very different from one another. Their shape, color, and fluffiness are affected by their height in the atmosphere, the temperature of the air, and the amount of water they're carrying.

Meteorologists study patterns in the weather. Using their knowledge of the climate and looking at readings from special equipment, they predict what the weather will be like over the next few weeks. Weather forecasts aren't always exact, but they're useful for warning people about potential dangers like storms, floods, and heat waves.

Climate change
Big shifts in temperature and weather patterns around the world are referred to as climate change. Over its long existence, our planet has experienced lots of changes. The Sun doesn't always send out the same amount of heat, and Earth wobbles as it moves through space. These natural factors have plunged Earth into long ice ages and caused land to change from forest to desert.

Humans are making climate change happen more quickly than it would naturally. Pollution from vehicles, farms, factories, and homes have added to the greenhouse effect, which traps heat in the atmosphere. This is melting icebergs, causing more extreme weather, and changing where plants and animals can live.

THE GREENHOUSE EFFECT

Our atmosphere has always trapped warmth from
the Sun, but pollution means that more and
more heat is being trapped.

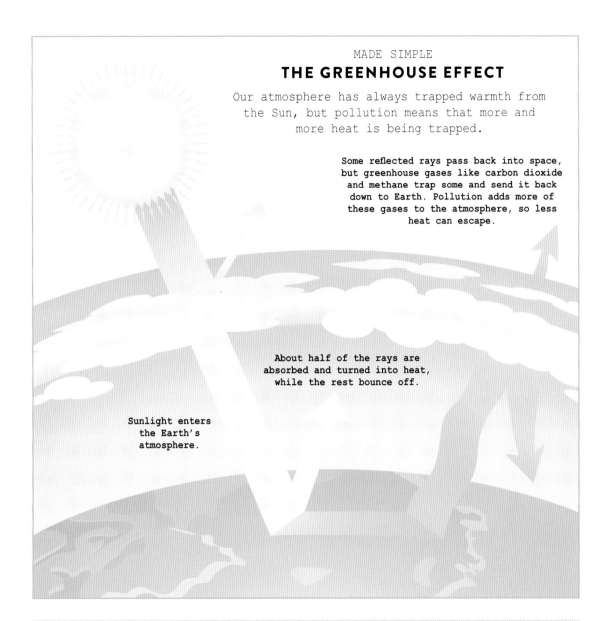

Some reflected rays pass back into space,
but greenhouse gases like carbon dioxide
and methane trap some and send it back
down to Earth. Pollution adds more of
these gases to the atmosphere, so less
heat can escape.

About half of the rays are
absorbed and turned into heat,
while the rest bounce off.

Sunlight enters
the Earth's
atmosphere.

ANSWER THIS

1. Which scientists study weather?

2. Are the conditions you can
   see right now the weather or
   the climate?

3. Which changes temperature
   faster—land or sea?

4. What makes air rise?

5. Name two examples of
   greenhouse gases.

EARTH SCIENCES

1. Where do convection currents occur?

a. The crust

b. The inner core

c. The mantle

d. The outer core

2. Which of these is not a type of plate boundary?

a. Conservative

b. Destructive

c. Defensive

d. Constructive

3. Which instrument detects and records earthquakes?

a. Voltmeter

b. Anemometer

c. Seismometer

d. Hydrometer

4. What is the name for molten rock inside the Earth?

a. Magma

b. Lahar

c. Meteor

d. Lava

5. Rain, snow, and hail are all types of...

a. Perspiration

b. Punctuation

c. Predation

d. Precipitation

6. Which of these causes biological weathering?

a. Rain

b. Plant roots

c. Changes in temperature

d. Waves

7. What is Earth's inner core made of?

a. Metal

b. Soil

c. Rock

d. Ice

8. How fast do tectonic plates move? As fast as...

a. Someone running

b. Fingernails growing

c. A snail

d. A train

9. Which of these does not cause climate change?

a. Pollution

b. Earth wobbling

c. Wind

d. Changes in the Sun's rays

10. Which layer of the atmosphere can living things breathe in?

a. Stratosphere

b. Troposphere

c. Exosphere

d. Mesosphere

Answers on page 212

SIMPLE SUMMARY

Once there was only empty space where Earth is now. It took billions of years and a remarkable series of events to create the planet we call home.

- The Earth's inner core is a ball of metal measuring about 1,520 miles (2,450 kilometers) across.

- As Earth grew, so did its gravitational pull, and for 500 million years the planet was pelted with lumps of matter that kept it hot and molten.

- The atmosphere has five layers and is made up of a combination of gases, plus other substances like dust and volcanic smoke that have risen up from the earth.

- Moving tectonic plates create mountains, earthquakes, and volcanoes as they move apart or bump into one other.

- When a volcano erupts, magma, gas, and ash burst out from the earth.

- Convection currents push tectonic plates until they move, with a jolt. The release of all the built-up energy can trigger an earthquake.

- The three types of rock are formed from combinations of minerals, which are natural solid substances made of one or more elements.

- Rocks are worn away by biological, chemical, and physical weathering.

- Water is constantly moving around the globe and being recycled in a process known as the water or hydrologic cycle.

- Big shifts in temperature and weather patterns around the world are referred to as climate change.

5
FORCES AND MOTION

All the things in the universe are either still or in motion. From the plane flying overhead to the chair you're sitting on, everything—whether it's moving or not—is affected by pushes, pulls, twists, stretches, and squashes known as forces.

WHAT YOU WILL LEARN

What is a force?

Motion

Gravity and weight

Friction and resistance

Torque and torsion

Stretching, squashing, and bending

Upthrust

Pressure

Magnets

5.1 WHAT IS A FORCE?

A force is a push or pull that makes an object change direction, shape, or speed. Forces are acting throughout the universe all the time—from the orbit of the Earth around the Sun to a boat sailing on the sea, everything is affected by forces.

Forces can be either applied or action-at-a-distance. Applied forces are exerted on one object by another, like a person kicking a ball, or bumper cars pushing one another. Action-at-a-distance forces, such as gravity and magnetism, can affect objects without actually touching them.

Forces are measured in newtons, shortened to N. One newton is the amount of force needed to accelerate a gram of matter by one centimeter per second squared. This sounds complicated, but it simply means that the stronger the push or pull, the higher the number of newtons.

PUSHING AND PULLING

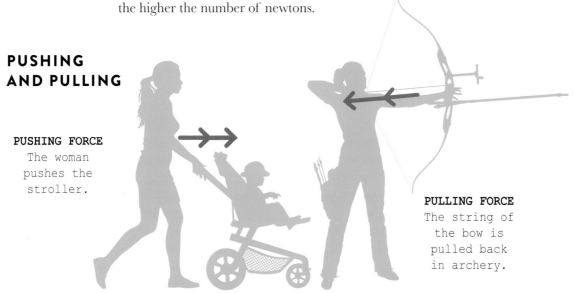

PUSHING FORCE
The woman pushes the stroller.

PULLING FORCE
The string of the bow is pulled back in archery.

FACT Due to all his important thinking and mathematical calculations, Isaac Newton has both a unit of measurement and a piece of equipment named after him. A newton meter measures force by measuring how much the spring inside it is stretched.

Balance

No force exists on its own; forces always work in pairs. If you perform an action like pushing a full shopping cart up a hill, there will be an opposite reaction as gravity tries to pull it back down. This is Newton's Third Law of Motion—you'll find out more about it in the next unit.

If an action and reaction are as strong as each other, the two forces acting in opposite directions cancel each other out and are said to be balanced. When forces are balanced, a still object will remain still and a moving object will carry on at the same speed.

ANSWER THIS

1. Which unit is used to measure forces?

2. What are the two types of forces?

3. Forces always work in _____.

4. Give two examples each of when you exerted pushing and pulling forces today.

MADE SIMPLE
BALANCED AND UNBALANCED FORCES

Imagine having a tug-of-war with someone the same size and strength as you; you can both pull as hard as you like but the rope won't move. If, however, the forces are unbalanced, like if your opponent is twice your size, stationary objects begin to move and moving objects change speed or direction.

400 N   BALANCED FORCE   400 N

400 N   UNBALANCED   300 N
                 FORCE

5.2 MOTION

Wave your arm above your head. You've just demonstrated motion. Motion is the movement of an object (or part of an object) from one place to another. Forces can affect an object's motion by changing the direction in which it's traveling and the speed at which it's moving.

There are several components that make up motion:

Distance How far an object travels
Speed How long it takes to move between one point and another
Velocity The speed an object travels in a particular distance
Acceleration How fast the object's speed increases

FACT

"Inertia" describes the tendency of an object to stay still or keep moving until its state is changed, as described in the First Law of Motion. When you stir a drink, the liquid keeps swirling after you've removed the spoon. The greater the mass of an object, the greater its inertia.

Some people get "motion sickness." It happens when the repetitive movements of a vehicle confuse the brain, and it can cause symptoms like dizziness and vomiting.

TYPES OF MOTION

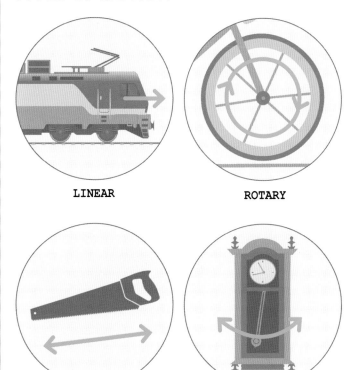

LINEAR

ROTARY

RECIPROCATING

OSCILLATING

Newton's laws of motion

Isaac Newton, the scientist who worked out that Earth's gravity pulls objects downward (see page 94), also came up with the laws of motion. These laws describe the way all objects move.

MADE SIMPLE
LAWS OF MOTION

FIRST LAW OF MOTION

Objects at rest stay at rest and objects in motion keep moving at the same speed and in the same direction, unless unbalanced forces act on them. A plate on a table will never move unless something moves it, and a tennis ball hit with a racket would keep flying in a straight line if gravity and air resistance didn't slow it and pull it down.

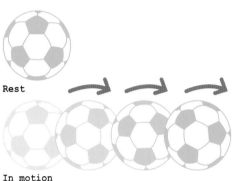

Rest

In motion

Kicking a football

Kicking a bowling ball

SECOND LAW OF MOTION

An object's acceleration depends on its mass and the strength of the force moving it. If you push a heavy object and a light object with the same amount of force, the motion of the light object will change more. You'd have to push harder to get the heavy object to accelerate at the same rate.

THIRD LAW OF MOTION

For every action there is an equal and opposite reaction. When you row a boat, your arms pull the oars and the oars push the water. When you throw a ball against a wall, the ball exerts a force on the wall, but the wall also exerts a force on the ball and makes it bounce back.

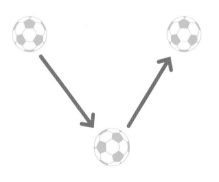

LESSON 5.3

GRAVITY AND WEIGHT

Things that go up always come back down. The famous story goes that Isaac Newton was sitting under a tree when he saw an apple fall to the ground. Rather than just picking it up and eating it, he began to wonder what made it fall down in the first place.

In 1687 Newton published his theory of gravity, explaining that every particle in the universe attracts every other particle. Gravity is the pulling force that keeps us on the ground. On a bigger scale, it's gravity that holds all the planets in our solar system in place. All objects have gravity, but most are too small for gravity to notice. The larger the mass of an object, the stronger its gravitational pull, which is why the Earth and the Sun have the power to pull other objects toward them. Gravity also gets stronger the closer you are to an object. Earth stays on its path around the Sun because the

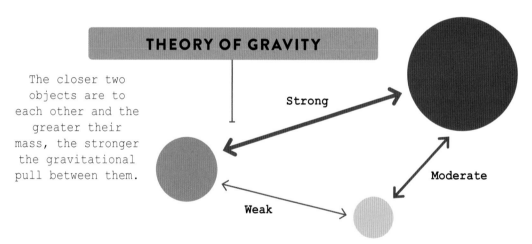

THEORY OF GRAVITY

The closer two objects are to each other and the greater their mass, the stronger the gravitational pull between them.

Strong

Moderate

Weak

ANSWER THIS

1. Which two factors affect the strength of an object's gravity?

2. How much would a person who weighs 100 pounds (45 kg) on Earth weigh on Mars?

3. Which planet in our solar system has the strongest gravity?

4. When was Newton's theory of gravity published?

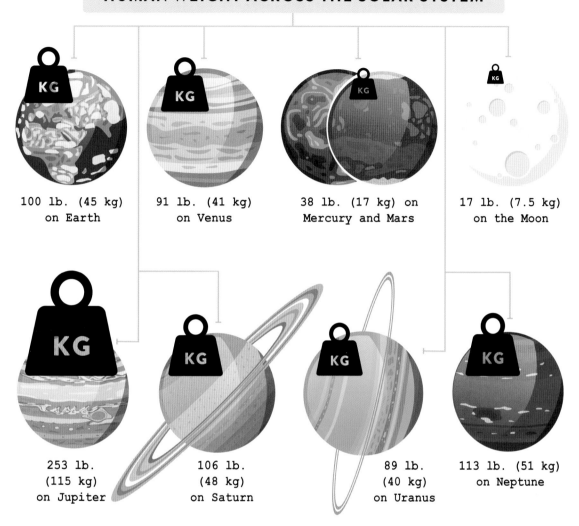

HUMAN WEIGHT ACROSS THE SOLAR SYSTEM

100 lb. (45 kg)
on Earth

91 lb. (41 kg)
on Venus

38 lb. (17 kg) on
Mercury and Mars

17 lb. (7.5 kg)
on the Moon

253 lb.
(115 kg)
on Jupiter

106 lb.
(48 kg)
on Saturn

89 lb.
(40 kg)
on Uranus

113 lb. (51 kg)
on Neptune

star's gravity stops our planet from moving any farther away. This is vital for life on Earth: if there was any more distance between us and the Sun, Earth would become too cold for anything to survive.

Weight

Mass is the number of atoms (see page 12) making up an object, and this number never changes. An object's weight is how hard it's being pulled by gravity; as different places and planets have different gravitational pulls, weight can change depending on where you are. On Jupiter, for example, you'd have the same mass as normal but weigh more than twice as much as you do on Earth. Astronauts in outer space can float around because the gravity there is very weak, making them weigh almost nothing.

LESSON 5.4

FRICTION AND RESISTANCE

If you've ever slid down a fire pole, shuffled across a floor, or pulled hard on a rope, you've felt friction. In fact, you experience friction every day; without it, things would be sliding all over the place around you. Friction is a sticking force that occurs when two surfaces try to slide past each other.

Friction works in the opposite direction to the way an object is trying to move, slowing it down or making it stop. The amount of friction acting on two surfaces depends on the materials they're made of. The rougher the surfaces, the more friction is generated; your shoes slide easily on ice, but you wouldn't get very far if you tried to glide on tarmac. Friction is often very useful—it allows you to grip the ground and walk without slipping, and means drivers can apply the brakes to slow down their cars.

When surfaces create friction, the energy they lose as they slow down is turned into heat—rub your hands together as quickly as you can and you'll feel them warm up. People surviving in the wild can use friction to light their campfires by rubbing sticks together, or by using a hard mineral called flint that creates sparks when it's struck against steel.

FACT

Sometimes we need to try and reduce friction so objects moving past each other don't get worn down, such as when adding oil to the moving parts in an engine or machine.

Fast-swimming animals like fish, dolphins, and sharks have smooth torpedo-shaped bodies that help reduce water resistance and make them streamlined. This shape, known as "fusiform," allows them to slide easily through the water.

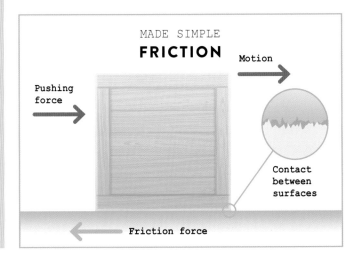

MADE SIMPLE
FRICTION

Motion

Pushing force

Contact between surfaces

Friction force

SURFACE FRICTION

SMOOTH SURFACES
> less friction

ROUGH SURFACES
> more friction

ANSWER THIS

1. Friction works in the
   _____ direction to
   a moving object.

2. Which type of surface
   produces the most
   friction?

3. What is another word
   for resistance?

4. Energy lost through
   friction turns into
   _____.

5. Shapes that minimize
   resistance are
   described as _____.

The drag of resistance

Resistance, or drag, is a kind of friction that acts against objects moving through gases and liquids. Flying objects like airplanes and kites experience air resistance as air particles in the sky hit them, and you'll have felt it if you've ever cycled really fast or ridden in a convertible car.

Water resistance occurs when something is floating on water or moving through it. If you try and walk through the water in a swimming pool, you'll find you're much slower than normal, because the water is pushing back against you with every step you take. Objects like rockets, planes, and speedboats are designed to move through air and water with as little resistance as possible—they're described as "streamlined."

AIR RESISTANCE

When a skydiver opens the parachute, air resistance works against gravity to slow the fall.

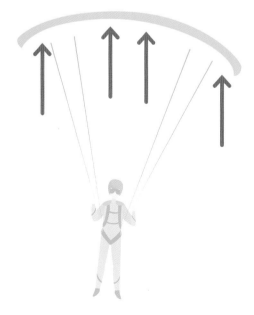

LESSON
5.5

TORQUE AND TORSION

Forces like gravity act in a straight line, giving objects "linear acceleration," but other forces can make objects turn and twist. These forces are said to give "angular acceleration."

Torque

Torque is an applied force that makes objects rotate (turn) around a fixed point called an axis or pivot. The turning effect of torque is called a moment. Think about pushing a door closed—you apply force to the handle, and the door swings away from you in an arc.

It's much easier to push a door at the side farthest from the hinges, even though you're applying force to the part that needs to move the most. When you increase the distance between the pivot and the point where force is applied, you increase the moment and produce a stronger turning effect. It's hard to unscrew a rusty bolt with your fingers; not only will you struggle to grip properly, it will also feel like you're just not strong enough to get it moving. Use a wrench with a long handle, though, and you'll be able to apply a much stronger force with less effort.

Torsion

While torque rotates a whole object in the same direction around one point, torsion is an applied twisting force that can cause parts of an object to rotate in opposite directions around different pivots. Imagine you're wringing out a wet towel—you turn one hand toward you and the other away to twist the cloth and squeeze out the water.

  FACT
Torsion can happen inside the human body, although it's rare. Organs can become twisted, limiting the amount of blood that can reach them. Organ torsion usually requires surgery.

IN PRACTICE

The longer the handle of the wrench, the bigger the "moment," and the easier it is to undo the bolt.

Depending on the material they're made of, objects can cope with different amounts of twisting. Materials like fabrics and rubber can be twisted many times and still return to their original shape, but materials like metal and wood will snap or shatter if too much torsion is applied.

ANSWER THIS

1. What is the effect of torque called?

2. Torsion is an _____ twisting force.

3. What is another word for an axis?

4. Torsion and torque give objects _____ acceleration.

STRETCHING, SQUASHING, AND BENDING

As well as changing its speed and direction, forces sometimes change an object's shape. A sudden change in speed or the application of a strong force can stretch, bend or squash, but there's only so much an object can take.

A change in shape caused by a force is called deformation. Bending, stretching ("extension"), and squashing ("compression") are all types of deformation. An object can undergo multiple types of deformation at once when several forces are acting on it.

Some objects are much more likely to undergo deformation than others. It takes an immense force to change the shape of a solid block of steel, and a boulder would shatter rather than be squashed; but you can squash a foam ball with the palm of your hand then watch it spring back to its original shape. Objects that can be easily deformed are described as flexible, elastic, or pliable, while those that hold their shape are rigid. Changes in shape that can be reversed when the force is removed are called elastic deformations.

FACT

The part of a trampoline that you jump on is attached to the frame with lots of springs. When you land, your weight makes the springs stretch downward, and when they return to their original shape, the force pushes you up into the air.

SQUASH AND STRETCH

A bouncing ball becomes squashed as it hits the floor, then stretches out as it bounces away.

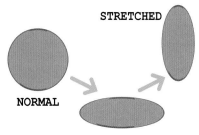

Hooke's law

The physicist Robert Hooke wrote a law to describe what usually happens when a flexible object is stretched or squashed. Hooke's law states that the deformation of an object or material increases as the force applied to it increases in strength. This is why the harder you pull an elastic band the longer it gets and if you double the force pulling on a spring, it should end up twice the length.

No matter how pliable or elastic an object is, there is always a limit to how much deformation it can withstand. When this "elastic limit" is reached, the object will either snap or become unable to return to its original shape. This permanent change is known as an inelastic deformation.

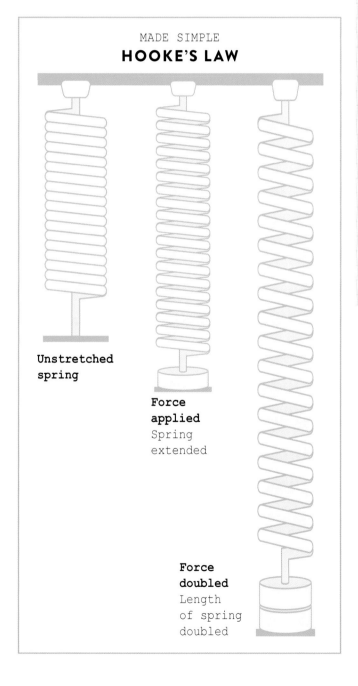

MADE SIMPLE
HOOKE'S LAW

Unstretched spring

Force applied
Spring extended

Force doubled
Length of spring doubled

ANSWER THIS

1. Stretching, squashing, and bending are all types of _____.

2. What is another word for squashing?

3. What would happen to the length of a spring if you tripled the force acting on it?

4. Who came up with a law about force and deformation?

5. Which three words can describe an object that changes shape easily?

5.7 UPTHRUST

Why do some objects float and others sink? The answer lies with upthrust, a force that works against gravity to try and hold objects on the surface of a liquid. Upthrust is an upward pushing force created because the pressure is greater at the bottom of the liquid than at the top. It's this push that makes you feel lighter in water than you do on dry land.

If gravity pulls down on an object more strongly than water can push it up, the object will sink. If the object's weight (and therefore the gravity acting on it) is equal to or less than the upthrust, it will float. Objects that float are described as being buoyant.

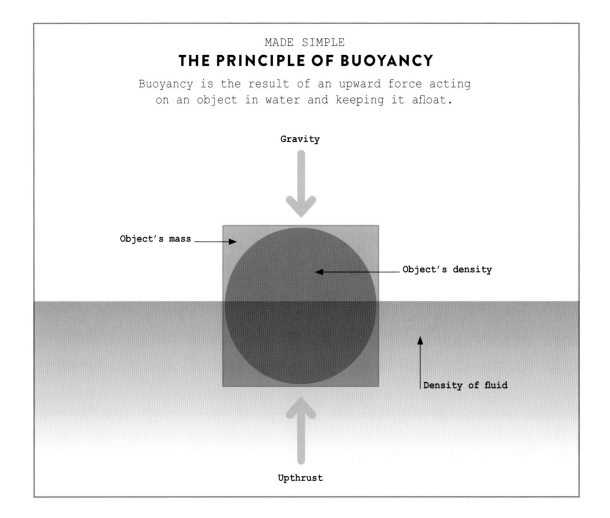

MADE SIMPLE
THE PRINCIPLE OF BUOYANCY
Buoyancy is the result of an upward force acting on an object in water and keeping it afloat.

Gravity

Object's mass

Object's density

Density of fluid

Upthrust

As well as weight, the density of the object and the liquid (how tightly packed all their particles are) affects buoyancy. If the object is more dense than the liquid it's placed in, the liquid won't be able to produce enough upthrust to hold its weight. A piece of cork has a low density because it's full of tiny air holes, so it will float on water, whereas a glass marble the same size will sink.

WATER DISPLACEMENT

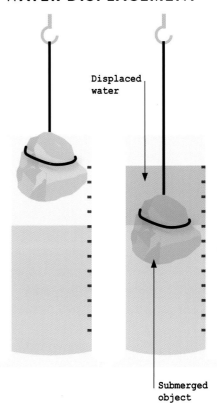

Displaced water

Submerged object

Archimedes' principle

According to legend, the ancient Greek mathematician Archimedes figured out how buoyancy works when he took a bath. He noticed that the water level rose when he got into the bath and fell when he got out. This is called displacement: when an object is submerged in water it pushes liquid out of the way and takes its place. The volume of liquid displaced is always the same as the volume of the submerged object.

Archimedes worked out that upthrust is equal to the weight of the liquid that has been displaced. It's as if the water is trying to move back into the space now taken up by the object.

ANSWER THIS

1. If gravity is stronger than upthrust, an object will _____.

2. Which two factors affect an object's buoyancy?

3. How do boats stay afloat?

4. Who came up with the idea of water displacement?

5. The volume of water displaced is equal to _____.

5.8 PRESSURE

People often say they're "under a lot of pressure" when they're stressed or have too much to do. This saying comes from the scientific concept of pressure, which describes the amount of force acting on an object.

Pressure is a word used to describe the force acting over a specific area. The smaller the area the force acts on, the greater the pressure. Imagine someone wearing sneakers stepped on your foot. Now imagine the same person stepped on your foot while wearing stiletto heels. The heel would hurt a lot more because the same amount of force is being applied over a much smaller area, so the pressure is greater.

There's a mathematical formula for working out pressure:
Pressure = Force ÷ Area

Pressure is usually measured in pascals, a unit named after French mathematician and physicist Blaise Pascal. It can also be measured using newtons per square meter or pounds per square inch.

Air pressure
Air puts pressure on the objects below it. Air pressure is the weight of all the gas above an object, pushing down on a particular surface. Objects higher up in Earth's atmosphere—for example, a rock at the top of a mountain—are under less air pressure because there's less air above them.

The power of pressure
Pressure has the power to change objects. Temperature often causes things to change between solid, liquid, and gas, but pressure impacts state too. Pressure inside the Earth can turn rocks from one type to another (see page 78), and the weight of all the other layers pushing down keeps the inner core solid, despite its high temperature. The higher the pressure something's under, the more heat energy is needed to change its state; water boils at 212°F (100°C) at sea level but turns to steam at a lower temperature on a mountain.

ANSWER THIS

1. Which unit is pressure most often measured in?

2. The smaller the area, the _____ the pressure.

3. Pressure can cause objects to change _____.

4. Which type of pressure is lower at the top of Everest?

5. High pressure keeps Earth's core _____.

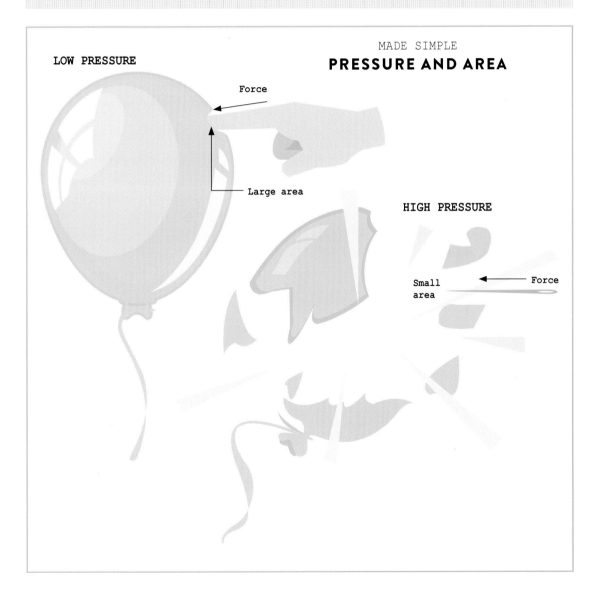

MADE SIMPLE
PRESSURE AND AREA

LOW PRESSURE

Force

Large area

HIGH PRESSURE

Small area

Force

5.9 MAGNETS

When someone is described as having a magnetic personality, it means that others are drawn to them and want to be around them. Real magnets can't tell jokes or flash a charming smile, but they do share the ability to pull things toward them.

Magnetism is an action-at-a-distance force created when electrons in the atoms that make up an object all spin in the same direction. Magnets are objects that create magnetic fields—areas of magnetic force—around themselves. These fields affect some metal objects (the ones made from cobalt, nickel, and iron) and other magnets, either pulling them closer or pushing them away.

Magnets come in different sizes and shapes, including horseshoe, bar, and round. Whatever its shape, every magnet has a north pole and a south pole, where its strongest forces are produced. If you cut a magnet in half, each piece will still have a north and south pole. These poles interact with the poles of other magnets and create pushing and pulling forces.

FACT

The strongest magnets in the known universe are stars called magnetars. These stars have magnetic fields trillions of times stronger than the Earth's, which distort and tear apart small planets and other space objects that get too close.

MADE SIMPLE
ATTRACTION AND REPULSION

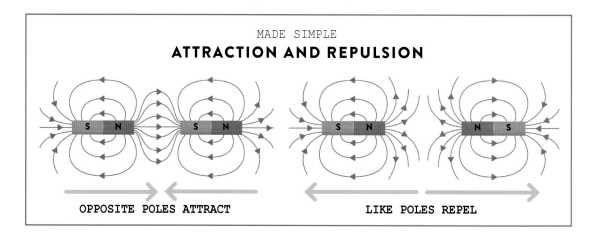

OPPOSITE POLES ATTRACT   LIKE POLES REPEL

Opposites attract

The north pole of a magnet attracts (pulls) the south pole of other magnets toward it. If you line up two bar magnets so the north pole of one faces the south pole of the other, they will move toward each other and feel like they're stuck together. The north pole of a magnet repels (pushes away) other north poles, and the south pole repels other south poles. If you turn one of the bar magnets around so the north poles are facing each other, they'll move apart, and it will be almost impossible to push them together.

EARTH'S MAGNETIC FIELD

The Earth is a giant magnet with its own North and South Poles.

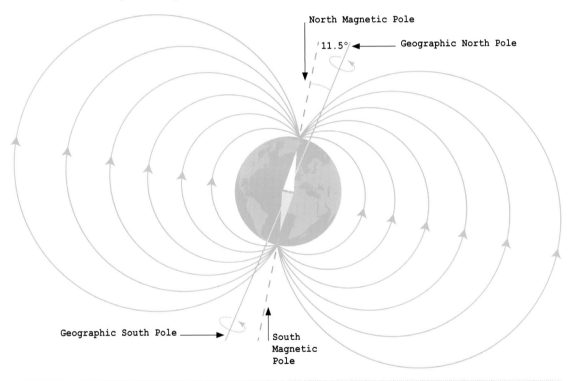

North Magnetic Pole

11.5° ← Geographic North Pole

Geographic South Pole → South Magnetic Pole

ANSWER THIS

1. Opposite poles always _____.

2. What sort of force is magnetism?

3. What type of star has the strongest magnetic field in the universe?

FORCES AND MOTION

1. Forces can be either action-at-a-distance or...

a. Appreciated

b. Applied

c. Appointed

d. Apparent

2. Upthrust is always equal to...

a. The weight of the liquid displaced by an object

b. The strength of gravity acting on an object

c. The volume of the object

d. The total volume of liquid

3. Which of these is not an example of oscillating motion?

a. A clock pendulum swinging

b. Someone rocking in a rocking chair

c. Someone using a saw

d. A child on a swing

4. Which force helps a skydiver slow down when they open their parachute?

a. Air resistance

b. Gravity

c. Upthrust

d. Torsion

5. What is the formula for calculating pressure?

a. Pressure = Force ÷ Area

b. Pressure = Area ÷ Weight

c. Pressure = Force x Area

d. Pressure = Force x Distance

6. What is an inelastic deformation?

a. A reversible change in shape

b. A temporary bending force

c. A constant twisting force

d. A permanent change in shape

7. Who came up with the theory of gravity?

a. Charles Darwin

b. Robert Hooke

c. Archimedes

d. Isaac Newton

8. What is the Third Law of Motion?

a. Every attraction causes a reaction

b. For every action there is an equal and opposite reaction

c. Every attraction has an equal and opposite repulsion

d. For every action there is another action

9. What causes magnetism?

a. Atoms all spinning in different directions

b. Atoms vibrating at high speed

c. Electrons all spinning in the same direction

d. Electrons moving slowly

Answers on page 213

SIMPLE SUMMARY

A force is a push or pull that makes an object change direction, shape, or speed. Forces affect an object's motion by changing the direction in which it's traveling and the speed at which it's moving.

• No force exists on its own; forces always work in pairs.

• The components that make up motion are distance, speed, velocity, and acceleration.

• Isaac Newton's theory of gravity explains that every particle in the universe attracts every other particle.

• An object's weight is how hard it's being pulled by gravity.

• Friction works in the opposite direction to the way an object is trying to move, slowing it down or making it stop.

• Resistance is a kind of friction that acts against objects moving through gases and liquids.

• Torque is an applied force that makes objects rotate around an axis or pivot; torsion is an applied twisting force that can cause parts of an object to rotate in opposite directions around different pivots.

• Bending, stretching, and squashing are all types of deformation, a force that causes an object to change shape.

• Upthrust works against gravity to try and hold objects on a liquid's surface.

• The smaller the area the force acts on, the greater the pressure.

• Magnetism is an action-at-a-distance force created when electrons in the atoms that make up an object all spin in the same direction.

6

ENERGY AND ELECTRICITY

Everything you do uses energy, from getting out of bed and turning on the light, to climbing up the stairs and brushing your teeth. Energy comes in many different forms, and humans have successfully harnessed some of them to power modern life.

WHAT YOU WILL LEARN

Types of energy

Energy transfer

Heating

Combustion

Electricity

Electrical circuits

Electricity in the home

Renewable and nonrenewable energy

TYPES OF ENERGY

When you have little energy you probably feel sleepy, but when you have lots of energy you're ready to learn and move and have fun. In physics, energy has a similar definition: it is the ability of an object to do work. This is usually measured in joules, sometimes shortened to J.

FACT The joule was originally invented as a unit for only measuring heat. It was named after John Prescott Joule, an English physicist and mathematician who spent years studying the nature of heat.

The total energy within a system—a set of things and the interactions between them—always remains the same, even if energy is moving around and changing form. Energy cannot be created or destroyed, it can only be stored or moved from one part of the system to another. This principle is called conservation of energy.

Energy comes in many different forms, including:
- **Kinetic** Found in all moving objects, from atoms to asteroids. The bigger the object and the faster it's moving, the more kinetic energy it has.
- **Gravitational potential** Stored by an object because of its position. A person about to go down a steep slide and a book about to fall off a shelf both have high potential energy.
- **Elastic** When an object is temporarily stretched or squashed, it stores enough energy to spring back to its original shape.
- **Heat** Also known as thermal energy. The hotter an object, the more thermal energy it has.
- **Light** Travels as electromagnetic waves, mostly from the Sun but also from objects like lamps. Our brains use light waves to build up a picture of the world around us.
- **Sound** Vibrations that travel through a medium and create sound when they reach our ears (see page 42).
- **Chemical** Comes from the reactions between molecules and atoms.
- **Nuclear** Released when atoms are split apart.
- **Electrical** Caused by the movement of electrons (see page 120). Electrical energy creates lightning and can be sent down wires as electricity.

TYPES OF ENERGY

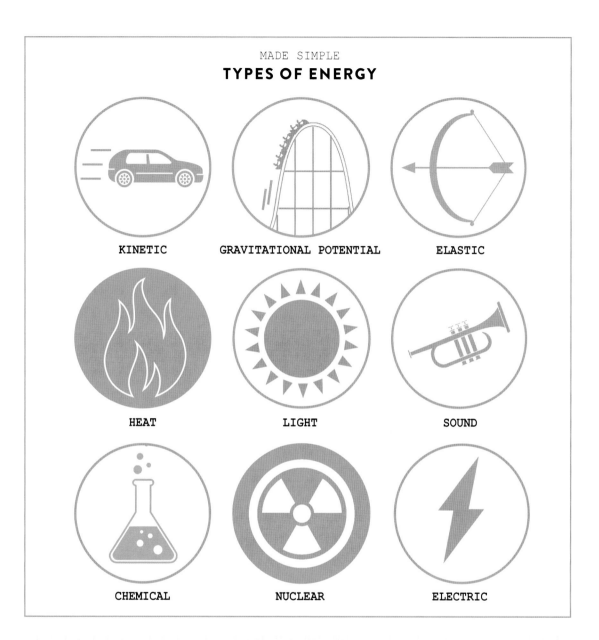

KINETIC	GRAVITATIONAL POTENTIAL	ELASTIC
HEAT	LIGHT	SOUND
CHEMICAL	NUCLEAR	ELECTRIC

ANSWER THIS

1. What sort of energy does a stretched spring have?

2. What unit of measurement is used to measure energy?

3. Imagine you hold an object above your head—what sort of energy does it have?

4. Energy cannot be ___ or ____.

ENERGY TRANSFER

We've seen that energy cannot be created or destroyed, and that it moves around a system. When energy moves from one place to another or changes form, it's known as an energy transfer.

When you turn on a TV, there is an energy transfer as electrical energy is turned into light and sound. Your digestive system converts food into energy your body can use. When a book gets knocked off a high shelf, its potential energy turns into kinetic energy.

Types of transfer

There are many ways for energy to be transferred. Some of the most common are:

- **Heating** When a hot object transfers some of its energy to a cooler object, warming it up.
- **Electrical transfer** When an electrical circuit is complete, energy can flow around it from the source and be turned into other useful forms.
- **Mechanical transfer** When the movement of one object moves another. Mechanical waves (see page 30) are also a type of mechanical energy transfer.
- **Radiation** Electromagnetic waves (see page 32) can transfer energy without moving through a medium like air or water.

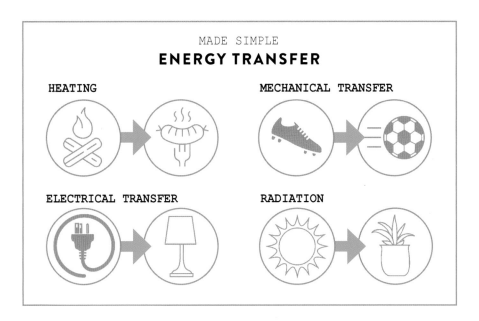

MADE SIMPLE
ENERGY TRANSFER

HEATING

MECHANICAL TRANSFER

ELECTRICAL TRANSFER

RADIATION

SANKEY DIAGRAM

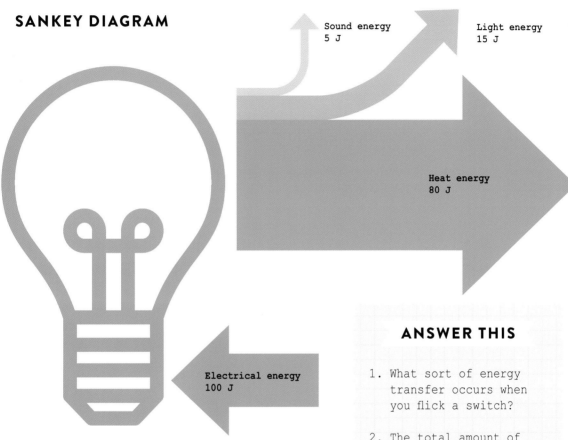

Sound energy
5 J

Light energy
15 J

Heat energy
80 J

Electrical energy
100 J

Waste

Energy transfer isn't always 100 percent efficient—some is usually "wasted" and turned into a form that doesn't help an object do its work. For example, a lightbulb gives off heat and a quiet buzzing sound as well as light. A Sankey diagram can be used to show all the energy transfers that happen when energy is released from a store. The width of the arrows shows how much energy is flowing along each path. No matter how many paths the energy goes down, the total of all the transfers will always equal the energy given out by the store.

ANSWER THIS

1. What sort of energy transfer occurs when you flick a switch?

2. The total amount of energy transferred is always _____ to the energy released from the store.

3. Which type of diagram can be used to show energy flow?

4. Radiation transfers energy without needing to travel through a _____.

6.3 HEATING

Temperature is a measure of how hot or cold something is. It's largely due to the movement or vibration of the particles that make up the object—the more energy they have, the faster they move, and the more energy is turned into heat.

If two objects close to each other are different temperatures, energy will be transferred from the hotter object until they are the same. The hot object cools down, while the cooler object gets warmer. When there is no longer a difference in temperature, the two objects have reached "thermal equilibrium" (a balance in temperature) and no more energy is transferred. This is how a hot water bottle works; heat from the bottle is transferred to your body, warming you up while the bottle gradually cools down.

Heat transfer
Thermal energy can be transferred between objects through conduction, convection, or radiation. Conduction occurs when the objects are touching—the fast-moving particles in the hot object bump into the particles of the cooler object, passing over some of their energy and making them vibrate faster. Some materials, like metal, are better conductors than others.

THERMAL ENERGY TRANSFER

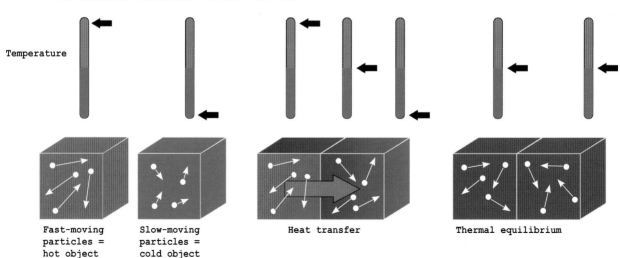

Temperature

Fast-moving particles = hot object

Slow-moving particles = cold object

Heat transfer

Thermal equilibrium

Particles in the cold object speed up while particles in the hot object begin to slow down.

Substances that are poor conductors are known as insulators.

In liquids and gases, the particles are free to move around. When particles with lots of energy move into a spot where low-energy particles were, heat is transferred to this new place. This is known as convection, and it's this process that creates convection currents in the Earth's mantle and moves tectonic plates (see page 74).

The third type of heat transfer is radiation. Unlike conduction and convection, this doesn't require the movement of particles; heat leaves an object as infrared waves (see page 32). The hotter an object, the more infrared waves it radiates. This is how the Sun's heat reaches us across millions of miles of space.

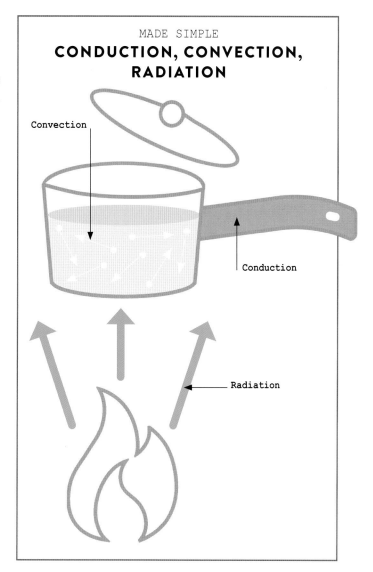

MADE SIMPLE
CONDUCTION, CONVECTION, RADIATION

Convection

Conduction

Radiation

ANSWER THIS

1. The faster the particles in an object are moving, the _____ its temperature.

2. What is another name for heat energy?

3. Which type of heat transfer occurs when high-energy particles move around in a liquid?

6.4 COMBUSTION

Combustion is the scientific term for burning. It's a reaction that takes place when a substance reacts with oxygen in the air and turns stored energy into light and heat energy. A reaction that gives out heat is known as exothermic.

There are three things needed for combustion to start and then keep going: fuel, oxygen, and heat. Together they make up the fire triangle (or "combustion triangle"). If you remove one of these components, the combustion stops; when you blow out birthday candles, the fast-moving breath removes heat by blowing the hot gases away from the wick. Firefighters tackle flames by using water or fire extinguishers to cool the fire, throwing sand or a fire blanket to remove the oxygen, or carefully removing any unburned fuel before it ignites. Not only is oxygen essential for combustion to begin, it also affects how something combusts. Depending on the amount of oxygen available, combustion happens in one of two ways.

Complete combustion

When there's plenty of oxygen available to react with the substance, the combustion is said to be complete. In complete combustion, the reaction produces carbon dioxide and water vapor as well as heat and light. The flame produced by the reaction is a vibrant blue.

FACT

Occasionally there are reports of people suddenly bursting into flames for no apparent reason. This phenomenon is called spontaneous human combustion. Some believe it's a result of energy inside the body, but many think the real cause is just never found, because it gets burned and destroyed.

COMBUSTION TRIANGLE

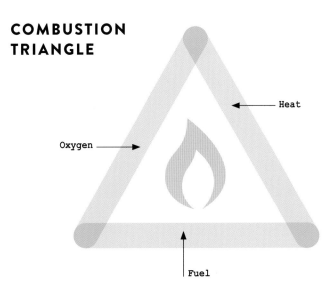

Heat

Oxygen

Fuel

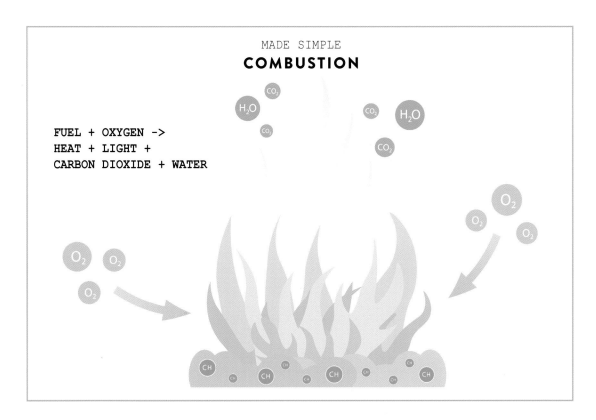

MADE SIMPLE
COMBUSTION

FUEL + OXYGEN ->
HEAT + LIGHT +
CARBON DIOXIDE + WATER

Incomplete combustion

There isn't always enough oxygen available for complete combustion. When this happens, incomplete combustion takes place. Incomplete combustion still produces carbon dioxide and water vapor, but it also produces carbon monoxide and pure carbon. Tiny particles of carbon—either produced by incomplete combustion or found in the fuel—glow red-hot, making the flames orange. Carbon monoxide is a colorless toxic gas with no smell. Faulty heaters in houses can sometimes produce dangerous amounts of it through incomplete combustion—the gas makes the people inside very sleepy and can eventually lead to death, so it's important that homes have carbon monoxide detectors to warn people if they're in danger.

ANSWER THIS

1. What are the products of complete combustion?

2. Which part of the fire triangle do you remove when you blow on a candle?

3. Which word describes a reaction that gives out heat?

4. It's hard to detect carbon monoxide gas because it has no _____.

LESSON
6.5 ELECTRICITY

Everything in the universe is made of atoms—particles so small that there are billions making up one coin. Tiny negatively charged particles called electrons whizz around the outside of atoms, usually kept from flying off by the pull of the positively charged protons at the atom's center. Sometimes, though, the electrons of some elements can come loose and jump over to another atom, leaving the atom with a positive "electrical charge."

When many electrons start jumping from atom to atom in the same direction, this creates the flow of energy that we know as electricity.

Current, voltage, and power

Just like the currents in an ocean, electric charge flows from place to place. Electrical currents will only flow if there is an energy source and a complete path for them to move along. The electricity inside a wire travels as a current, and so does the electrical energy in a lightning bolt. Current is measured in amperes (or just "amps"), based on how much electricity flows past a particular point in one second.

CONDUCTOR

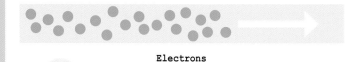

Electrons

Water

Electricity moves along a conductor like water flowing through a hose.

Voltage is the force that makes electrons flow. Measured in volts, it's calculated by finding the difference in charge between two points on a circuit. Electricity moves from points with high voltage (like a battery) to places with lower voltage. Power used by a circuit is measured in watts, worked out by multiplying the current by the voltage.

Conductors and insulators

Metals like copper are good conductors for making wires, because their electrons aren't held tightly and can jump to other atoms. Electricity can't flow through insulators like rubber and plastic, which are said to have high resistance, so they're used to cover wires and components.

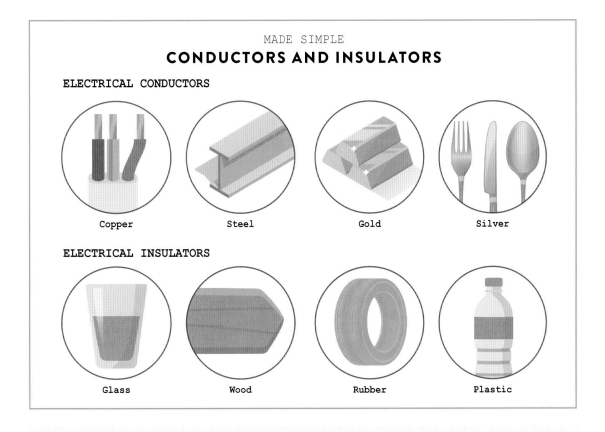

MADE SIMPLE

CONDUCTORS AND INSULATORS

ELECTRICAL CONDUCTORS

Copper   Steel   Gold   Silver

ELECTRICAL INSULATORS

Glass   Wood   Rubber   Plastic

ANSWER THIS

1. Which unit is used to measure current?

2. Energy moves from areas of _____ voltage to areas of _____ voltage.

3. Is fabric an electrical conductor or insulator?

4. Insulating materials are said to have high _____.

ELECTRICAL CIRCUITS

Every time you turn on a light, a computer, or a microwave, you're controlling an electrical circuit. These loops of wire and electrical components bring an electrical current to the object you want to use, delivering the power it needs to do its job.

Electricity flows around circuits from an energy source with high voltage to areas with low voltage, interacting with components on its way round to complete a task. Energy can only flow when there is a complete loop (or "closed circuit")—if the circuit is broken the current reaches a dead end and can't go any further. All circuits must have wires and a power source to work

MADE SIMPLE
ELECTRIC CIRCUIT SYMBOLS

CELL
A simple electrical power supply holding stored energy

BATTERY
Two or more cells joined together

SWITCH
Turns a circuit on and off by completing the loop or breaking the flow of electricity

LOAD
The object or appliance the circuit is powering, like a bulb or buzzer

RESISTOR
Limits the flow of the electrical current; a fixed resistor's resistance is always the same, but a variable resistor can be altered

CONDUCTORS
Wires that connect the other components

SERIES AND PARALLEL CIRCUITS

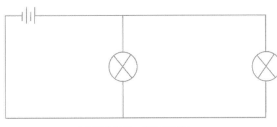

SERIES CIRCUIT

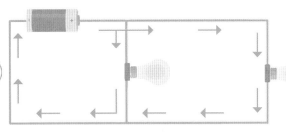

SERIES CIRCUIT

PARALLEL CIRCUIT

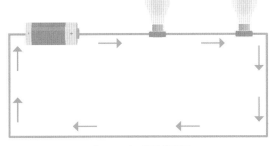

PARALLEL CIRCUIT

properly, but the other components depend on what the circuit is being used for.

Making connections

There are two ways to connect the components in a circuit. In a series circuit, all the components are linked in one simple loop and there is only one way the current can flow. In a parallel circuit, there are multiple paths for the electricity to move along. Parallel circuits are used when there are lots of components. If one branch of a parallel circuit is broken, energy can still find a complete loop to flow around, so some components will continue to work.

ANSWER THIS

1. Why are wires covered in insulation?

2. Wires _____ the other components in the circuit.

3. Give an example of a load.

4. Which type of circuit has multiple pathways?

ELECTRICITY IN THE HOME

You now know how electricity works and you know that it powers electrical items in your home, but how does it get there? Try to imagine millions of electrons flowing like water in a hose as you follow the journey electricity goes on to get from generator to games console.

Electricity is produced at power plants (also known as power stations or generating stations). Large devices called generators use energy from sources like wind, oil, and coal to spin a magnet. Turning the magnet creates a magnetic field that pulls electrons from their atoms and sends them flowing along a wire.

The electric current heads out of the generator and travels along wires to a step-up transformer. The transformer increases the voltage and decreases the current, which helps the electricity to flow over a long distance. Electric power lines (or "transmission lines") attached to tall metal towers transport the electricity hundreds of miles toward its destination.

Once it's close to your house, another transformer reduces the voltage and increases the current so it can travel down smaller wires. Transmission lines branch off into "distribution lines" that take electricity to each neighborhood. Small transformers decrease the voltage even more so it's safe for use in the home. Once the electricity is safe and ready, wires deliver it to the circuits inside your house.

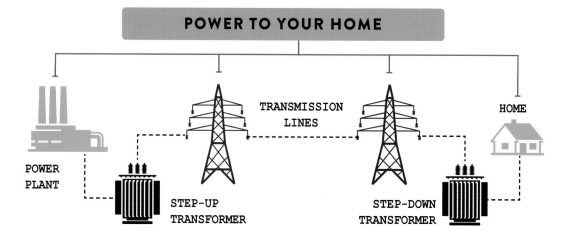

POWER TO YOUR HOME

TRANSMISSION LINES

HOME

POWER PLANT

STEP-UP TRANSFORMER

STEP-DOWN TRANSFORMER

Electricity costs money, and can lead to pollution if it's generated using fossil fuels (see page 126). There are lots of easy ways to save electricity around the home:

SAVING ELECTRICITY

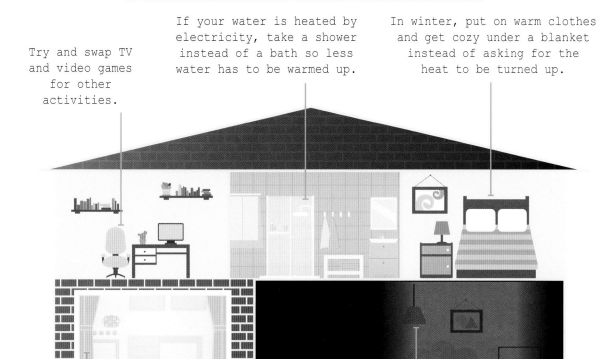

Try and swap TV and video games for other activities.

If your water is heated by electricity, take a shower instead of a bath so less water has to be warmed up.

In winter, put on warm clothes and get cozy under a blanket instead of asking for the heat to be turned up.

Open your curtains instead of turning on a light in the daytime.

Turn off lights when you leave a room, and switch off devices and chargers at the plug when you're not using them.

ANSWER THIS

1. What is the name of the device that produces electricity?

2. What should you do when you leave a room?

3. Which type of transformer increases voltage?

4. Why does voltage have to be decreased before entering a home?

5. Why does swapping a bath for a shower save electricity?

LESSON 6.8

RENEWABLE AND NONRENEWABLE ENERGY

We use lots of different sources for our energy, which can be divided into two categories: renewable and nonrenewable. Renewable energy sources can be replaced and will not run out, but nonrenewable sources are gone once they've been used up.

Nonrenewable energy

Lots of energy comes from burning fossil fuels—coal, oil, and gas. Most vehicles run on fossil fuels, which are used to create electricity too. Formed over millions of years from the remains of dead plants and animals, the sources are extracted from the ground and then transported around the world. As well as being a finite resource, burning fossil fuels creates pollution.

Nuclear energy is the energy held inside an atom by the forces that keep it together. Scientists worked out how to split atoms apart and release all the energy inside, in a process known as nuclear fission. At nuclear power stations, millions and millions of atoms (usually from the elements uranium and plutonium) are broken apart to release heat energy. The heat from this process is used to turn water into steam, and the steam rises and turns turbines that generate electricity. There's only so much uranium and plutonium on Earth, and nuclear fission creates toxic radioactive materials.

Renewable energy

New renewable sources are being created and tested as new technology is invented, but the main types include:

- **Solar energy** Solar panels in fields and on the roofs of buildings collect energy from the Sun's rays and turn it into power.
- **Wave energy** Machines called "wave energy converters" capture the power of ocean waves.
- **Wind energy** Tall turbines are spun by the wind, and this movement turns a generator.
- **Hydroelectric power** When water held behind a dam is allowed to flow down to a river or lake below, the kinetic energy of the rushing water drives generators.
- **Geothermal energy** Hot water and steam rising from deep inside the Earth can be used to turn turbines.

MADE SIMPLE
RENEWABLE AND NONRENEWABLE ENERGY

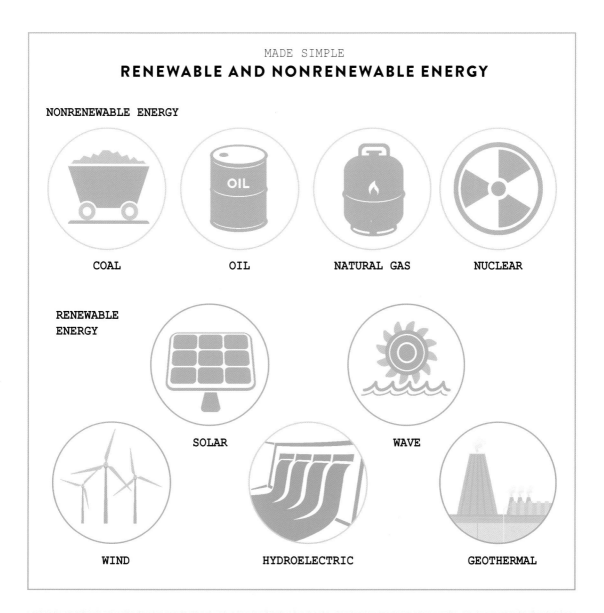

NONRENEWABLE ENERGY

COAL   OIL   NATURAL GAS   NUCLEAR

RENEWABLE ENERGY

SOLAR   WAVE

WIND   HYDROELECTRIC   GEOTHERMAL

ANSWER THIS

1. What are fossil fuels made of?

2. Renewable energy sources are sources that can be _____.

3. Which type of power is produced at a dam?

4. What is split apart to create nuclear energy?

ENERGY AND ELECTRICITY

1. Which type of energy transfer happens when one object moves another?
   a. Electrical
   b. Heating
   c. Radiation
   d. Mechanical

2. What is the name for energy that comes from the reactions between molecules and atoms?
   a. Chemical
   b. Nuclear
   c. Gravitational potential
   d. Electrical

3. A hot object transfers heat energy to a cooler object until they reach...
   a. Thermic balance
   b. Thermal equilibrium
   c. Thermic instability
   d. Thermal imbalance

4. Which three things make up the fire triangle?
   a. Fuel, fire, and oxygen
   b. Air, wood, and heat
   c. Matches, fuel, and air
   d. Oxygen, fuel, and heat

5. Which type of heat transfer allows warmth from the Sun to reach us?
   a. Convection
   b. Radiation
   c. Conduction
   d. Radius

6. Which of these is not a renewable energy source?
   a. Coal
   b. Wind
   c. Water
   d. Solar

7. Electric current is created by the movement of _____.
   a. Batteries
   b. Atoms
   c. Wires
   d. Electrons

8. Complete combustion gives a _____ flame.
   a. Yellow
   b. Blue
   c. Orange
   d. Green

9. Which type of circuit only has one path for electricity to flow along?
   a. Parallel
   b. Simple
   c. Series
   d. Parting

10. Which of these is not a good way to save electricity?
    a. Wear a sweater instead of turning on the heat
    b. Hang clothes out to dry instead of using a dryer
    c. Leave the fridge door open once you've got your food out
    d. Turn off electrical items when you're not using them

Answers on page 214

SIMPLE SUMMARY

Energy comes in many different forms, which we have harnessed to power our modern lifestyles.

- Energy cannot be created or destroyed, it can only be stored or moved from one part of the system to another.

- When energy moves from one place to another or changes form, it's known as an energy transfer.

- Thermal energy can be transferred between objects through conduction, convection, or radiation.

- Fuel, oxygen, and heat make up the combustion triangle.

- When there's plenty of oxygen available to react with a substance, the combustion is complete; when there isn't enough oxygen available, the combustion is incomplete.

- An electrical current is created by the movement of electrons.

- Electricity flows around circuits from an energy source with high voltage to areas with low voltage, interacting with components on its way round to complete a task.

- Generators use energy from sources like wind, oil, and coal to spin a magnet. Turning the magnet creates a magnetic field that pulls electrons from their atoms and sends them flowing along a wire, eventually reaching your home in the form of electricity.

- Renewable energy sources can be replaced and will not run out, but nonrenewable sources are gone once they've been used up.

7
STATES AND CHANGES

Imagine a lake on a warm summer's day. Now imagine the same lake in the middle of a cold winter. Whatever the time of year, the lake is filled with the same substance—water—so why is it perfect for swimming in one season and ice-skating in another?

WHAT YOU WILL LEARN

Solids, liquids, and gases

Density

Diffusion

Freezing and melting

Boiling, evaporation, and condensation

Sublimation and deposition

Mixtures and solutions

SOLIDS, LIQUIDS, AND GASES

Everything in the universe is made of matter. Matter exists in many different forms, depending on the conditions it's under, but on Earth it's mostly found in three states: solid, liquid, and gas. Each state has a unique set of properties.

Solids

Solids are made of particles packed tightly in a uniform pattern. The particles can vibrate on the spot, but strong bonds between them mean they can't move out of their formation. Because of this, solids hold their shape and don't flow or spread out to fill a space. Solids can be cut and carved, but most cannot be compressed.

THE THREE STATES OF MATTER

SOLID	LIQUID	GAS
• Fixed shape	• No fixed shape	• No fixed shape
• Fixed volume	• Fixed volume	• No fixed volume
• Particles close together	• Particles close together	• Particles far apart
• Does not flow easily	• Flows easily	• Flows easily

FACT
Gas particles in a container bump into one another and the container walls as they move around in different directions. This creates pressure. When the temperature of a gas is increased, the particles have more energy, move faster, and collide with the walls more frequently, which increases the pressure.

Liquids

The particles in liquids are also close together, but they're more randomly arranged and held by weaker bonds. This gives them the freedom to move around, meaning that liquids can flow and will change shape to fit a container. Liquids can't be squashed—while they change shape, they always take up the same amount of space.

Gases

Gas particles are randomly distributed with lots of space between them. This means that as well as flowing, gases can expand and be compressed. Most gases easily escape from containers and spread out in the air, unless they are tightly sealed. Another property of gases is that they are often invisible—several different gases make up the air in the Earth's atmosphere (see page 72), none of which we can see.

Solid or liquid?

A block of wood, a glass of juice, and the air inside a balloon can easily be put into one of these categories, but what about things like sand and sugar? These substances can be poured and change shape to fit a container, matching some of the properties of a liquid. In fact, they're made up of thousands of tiny solids; each grain of sugar or sand has tightly packed rows of particles and always holds the same shape, but when they tumble over each other they create the impression that they are flowing.

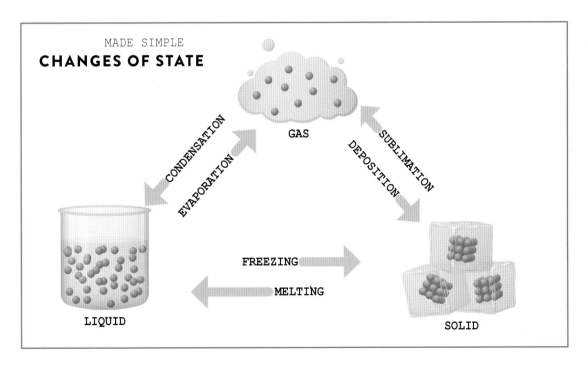

MADE SIMPLE
CHANGES OF STATE

CONDENSATION

EVAPORATION

GAS

SUBLIMATION

DEPOSITION

FREEZING

MELTING

LIQUID

SOLID

7.2 DENSITY

Imagine you're holding a container full of water in one hand and an equal-sized container filled with air in the other. Even though the volume is exactly the same, the container of water will feel much heavier. This is because the water and the air have very different densities.

The density of a substance or material is the amount of matter packed into a given space. The more dense, the heavier it feels for its size. Density is calculated using this equation:

DENSITY

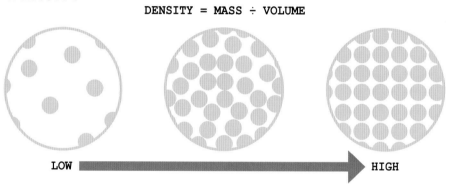

DENSITY = MASS ÷ VOLUME

LOW ➞ HIGH

The unit of density depends on the units used to measure the mass and volume; the density of a rubber ball might be written in g/cm^3 or oz/in^3, while it would make more sense for the density of an oak tree to be measured in kilos or tons per meter or foot cubed.

Solids usually have high densities because their particles are packed so tightly. Particles are also close together in liquids, making them almost as dense as solids. The particles in gases are far apart, giving them very low densities. This is why you don't feel the air around you unless it's windy.

FACT

Density can be affected by pressure (see page 104) and temperature. When a substance or material is under high pressure, its particles are forced closer together; its mass stays the same but its volume decreases. When the temperature decreases, the particles move less quickly and get closer together.

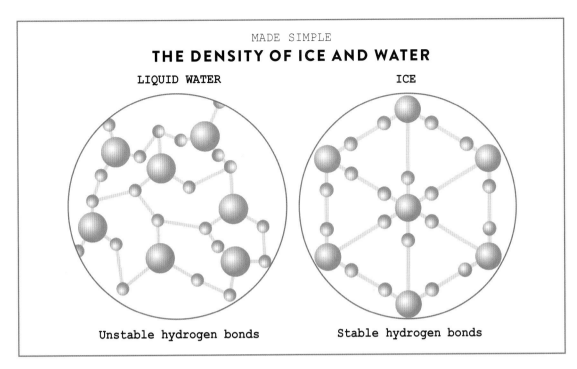

MADE SIMPLE
THE DENSITY OF ICE AND WATER

LIQUID WATER   ICE

Unstable hydrogen bonds   Stable hydrogen bonds

Weird water

Water, like other substances, is least dense in its gaseous state, but ice is less dense than liquid water. This strange behavior is caused by a special type of bond called a hydrogen bond that forms between the oxygen atom of one water molecule and a hydrogen atom of another. When water is liquid the molecules have lots of energy, so they break and reform the bonds and move around close to each other. When water gets colder, the bonds become more stable and harder to break. They hold the water molecules farther away from each other in an organized structure. This increases the volume of the water by almost 10 percent and reduces the density, which is why ice cubes bob around in a cool drink and huge icebergs can stay afloat on the sea.

ANSWER THIS

1. How do you calculate density?

2. Which state of matter is the least dense?

3. Density can be affected by _____ and _____.

4. Which type of bond holds water molecules apart in ice?

5. Which is more dense: oil or water?

7.3 DIFFUSION

When someone's cooking your favorite food in the kitchen, you can smell it even if you're in a different part of the house. You have a process called diffusion to thank for the delicious scent reaching your nose.

The particles in liquids and gases are free to move from one place to another. As they bump into each other they change direction and eventually spread out in a container or room. Diffusion doesn't happen in solids because their particles can't move around—they can only vibrate on the spot.

Substances move from areas of high concentration (lots of particles of the same type) to areas of low concentration (few or no other particles of the same type). When particles of a chemical are released, they disperse (spread out) and mix with the air. They spread from the high concentration in the spot where they were released to the low concentration areas in the rest of the space. The particles move until eventually they're evenly spread out.

Diffusion in liquid is slower than in gas because the particles don't move as quickly. Over time, though, the same process takes place and the liquid

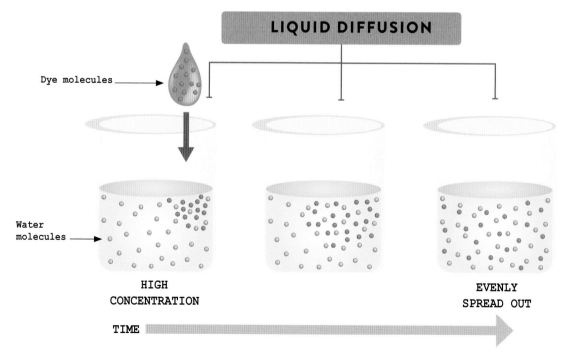

LIQUID DIFFUSION

Dye molecules

Water molecules

HIGH CONCENTRATION

EVENLY SPREAD OUT

TIME

particles spread out. If you pour orange juice or black currant squash into a glass of water, you can watch the cloud of colored liquid spread until all the liquid in the glass is the same color.

Diffusion in the body

When you take a breath in and air enters the lungs (see page 194), oxygen diffuses from tiny air sacs called alveoli to the bloodstream to be taken to cells around the body while carbon dioxide diffuses the other way. Cell walls let oxygen and other useful substances move into the center of the cell, but can put up barriers to stop other things from getting in.

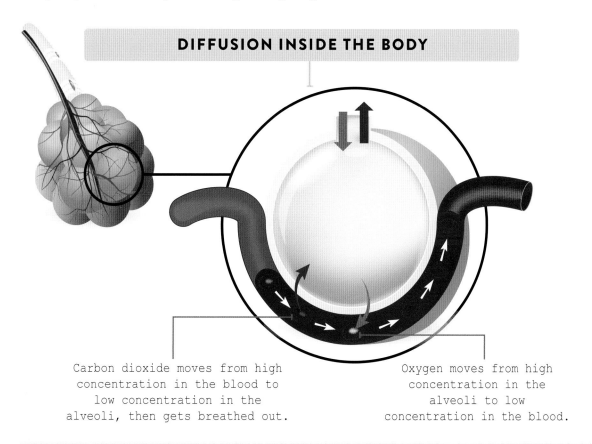

DIFFUSION INSIDE THE BODY

Carbon dioxide moves from high concentration in the blood to low concentration in the alveoli, then gets breathed out.

Oxygen moves from high concentration in the alveoli to low concentration in the blood.

ANSWER THIS

1. Why can't diffusion happen in solids?

2. Substances diffuse to areas of _____ concentration.

3. What does the word disperse mean?

FREEZING AND MELTING

Think about a cool glass of water with ice cubes. The liquid water and the ice are made of exactly the same molecules, they're just in different states because the ice is colder. Matter can be changed from liquid to solid and back again by freezing and melting.

As you've seen, the particles in a solid are held in a uniform structure by strong bonds. As the solid warms up, the particles vibrate faster and faster until they finally have enough energy to break the bonds and move around more freely. The temperature that allows a substance to change from a solid to a liquid is called its melting point.

When liquids are cooled, they lose heat energy. The molecules slow down and move around less. Eventually, the temperature reaches the substance's freezing point (the exact same temperature as the melting point) and the particles settle into neat rows and become a solid.

Different substances have different melting and freezing points. Water freezes when temperatures fall below 32°F (0°C) and melts at temperatures above this point. Mercury, a metal that used to be used inside thermometers, is a liquid above −37.9°F (−38.8°C), but gold doesn't melt until it reaches 1,943°F (1,064°C).

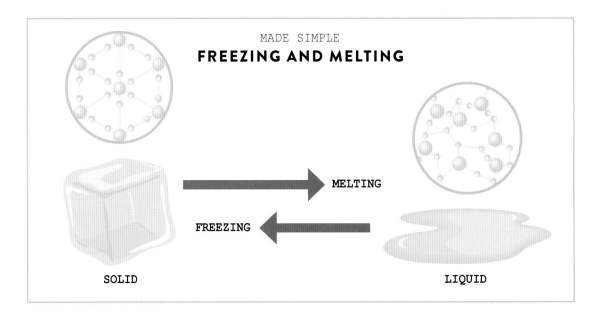

MADE SIMPLE
FREEZING AND MELTING

MELTING

FREEZING

SOLID

LIQUID

When substances change between liquid and solid, no matter is gained or lost—the mass is exactly the same in each state. If you were to weigh a jug of water then pour it into ice cube molds and freeze it, the ice cubes all together would weigh the same amount as the liquid you started with.

ANSWER THIS

1. What is the freezing point of water?

2. What happens to the movement of particles as temperature decreases?

3. How much matter is lost when something melts?

4. What is an irreversible change?

5. What state is mercury at room temperature?

MELTING POINTS

The candle melts as the wick burns, but the bronze candlestick doesn't melt, because bronze has a much higher melting point than wax.

BOILING, EVAPORATION, AND CONDENSATION

When you heat a pan of water, bubbles start to form. Keep heating it and eventually a plume of water vapor—also known as steam—begins to rise from the pan. This is boiling: the change of matter from liquid to gas. If the steam meets a cool window, little droplets of water form—this is condensation.

Boiling

When a liquid reaches a certain temperature, its molecules gain enough energy to break the weak bonds between them and become a gas. This change is called boiling or vaporization, and the particular temperature is the liquid's boiling point. Under normal pressure, water's boiling point is 212°F (100°C).

Human bodies sweat when they're too warm. The moisture is released from sweat glands and gathers on the skin. When the droplets evaporate, they each take away some heat from the body and cool the person down. Lots of mammals sweat a little bit, but only other primates (monkeys and apes) and horses sweat as much as humans.

Evaporation

Sometimes it's only the water at the surface of a liquid that turns into a gas. This is known as evaporation. Evaporation can happen at a lower temperature than boiling. It would take an incredible amount of energy to boil an ocean, but high-energy particles in the air can easily turn the water at the surface into a gas. This is how sea water and puddles end up moving into the sky and forming clouds (see page 82); rays from the Sun add enough energy to the molecules at the surface for a thin layer of water to turn into vapor.

Condensation

When gas cools, it turns to liquid. This change of state, condensation, is the opposite of boiling and evaporation. Condensation takes place when the temperature of a gas is decreased by cooler weather or refrigeration. It also happens when gas particles bump into a cold surface and cool suddenly, which is why condensation forms on windows and wall tiles.

On a cold day, you can see your breath in the air. This wispy cloud is created because the gas you breathe out contains a small amount of water vapor. When it meets the cold air, the vapor instantly condenses to form water droplets and some of these droplets freeze to create tiny ice crystals.

MADE SIMPLE
WATER BOILING, EVAPORATING, AND CONDENSING

Heat from the Sun

Cold window glass

BOILING   EVAPORATION   CONDENSATION

ANSWER THIS

1. What is another name for boiling?

2. Where in a liquid does evaporation happen?

3. What is the normal boiling point of water?

4. Which state change happens when you sweat?

SUBLIMATION AND DEPOSITION

Usually, matter changes from solid to liquid and then to a gas. Sometimes, though, the substance is put under a set of conditions that cause it to skip the liquid phase entirely. These changes are known as sublimation and deposition (desublimation).

FACT

Dry ice is carbon dioxide in its solid state. Carbon dioxide becomes a solid at -109.3°F (-78.5°C), so dry ice is often used for refrigerating things that need to be kept very cold. When dry ice warms up it sublimates from a solid into wisps of carbon dioxide gas, which is used in magic tricks or to create "fog" in movies.

Sublimation

Pressure has a big impact on matter and the state it's in—the center of the Earth doesn't melt or boil even though it's extremely hot, because the weight of all the layers above it press down and keep the atoms in the core close together. High up a mountain, the pressure in the atmosphere is lower than it is close to the sea. When low atmospheric pressure is combined with low humidity ("dry" air with little water vapor in it), strong sunlight and strong winds, snow and ice can turn straight into vapor without melting first. These very specific conditions are not met in other places, which is why snow on Mount Everest sublimates and seems to disappear into thin air, but snow in a town at sea level melts to leave roads and gardens covered in water.

SUBLIMATION

SUNLIGHT

WIND

VAPOR

SUBLIMATION

SNOW

Deposition

Deposition is the opposite of sublimation—it's a change straight from gas to solid. You'll have seen the result of deposition if you live somewhere that gets cold and frosty in the winter. Frost forms on things like leaves and cars when the temperature drops on a cold night. Water vapor in the air becomes supercooled, dropping below its condensation point and freezing point but remaining in its gaseous state. When molecules of supercooled vapor bump into a cold object, the water immediately changes from gas to liquid and forms a thin layer of ice crystals.

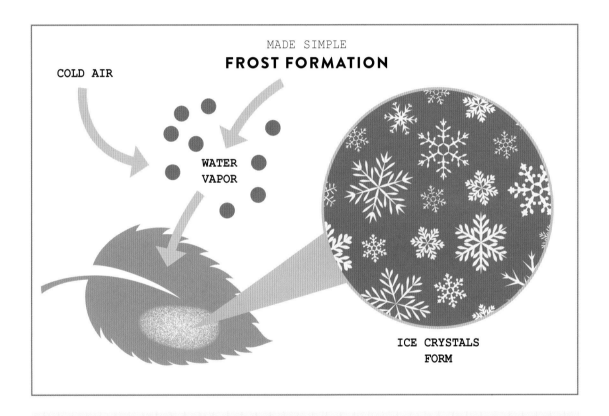

MADE SIMPLE
FROST FORMATION

COLD AIR

WATER VAPOR

ICE CRYSTALS FORM

ANSWER THIS

1. Where are you likely to see snow sublimating?

2. Which state do sublimation and deposition skip?

3. What can be used to create the illusion of fog?

4. Which change of state creates frost?

MIXTURES AND SOLUTIONS

Mixtures are created when two substances are combined but there's no chemical reaction between them. If you mix sand into water, no atoms are rearranged and no new substances are created—the sand is still sand and the water is still water; their molecules are just dispersed among one another. Unlike the product of a reaction, the different parts of a mixture can be separated again.

MIXTURE OR SOLUTION?

Water + sand

Water + salt

MIXTURE
• Different substances are easy to see
• Not always evenly mixed
• Can be separated by sieving or filtering

SOLUTION
• Impossible to see different substances
• Evenly mixed
• Cannot be separated by sieving or filtering

Substances that will form a mixture together are described as miscible, and those that won't mix are called immiscible. Water and lemon juice are miscible, but because of their different densities water and oil are immiscible—no matter how much you stir them, they will always separate into different layers.

Solutions

If you stir sugar into a glass of water, it will look like it has disappeared. The sugar is still there and will make the water taste sweet—it has dissolved into the water and made a mixture called a solution. A substance that dissolves is called a solute, and the substance it dissolves in is called a solvent.

FACT

There are two main types of mixture: homogeneous and heterogeneous. In a homogeneous mixture, like blood, air, or salt water, all the substances are evenly distributed. In a heterogenous mixture, such as soil or a salad, distribution is not even and you can see the different parts.

When a solute is added to a solvent, particles of both substances bump into one another. As they collide, the solvent particles move the particles of solute until they're spread out evenly. There's a limit to the amount of solute a volume of solvent can dissolve. Past this point, the solution is saturated and any solute added will stay separate from the mixture. Substances that dissolve in water are called soluble; substances that don't are called insoluble.

Separation

There are several ways of separating mixtures and solutions, including:

• **Sieving** Mixtures of different-sized dry solids can be separated with a sieve. Sieving also works for large solids mixed with liquids, like pieces of gravel in water.
• **Filtering** Filter paper has much smaller holes than a sieve, so it can be used to separate mixtures like sand and water.
• **Evaporation** If you boil away the solvent in a solution, the dissolved solid will be left behind.

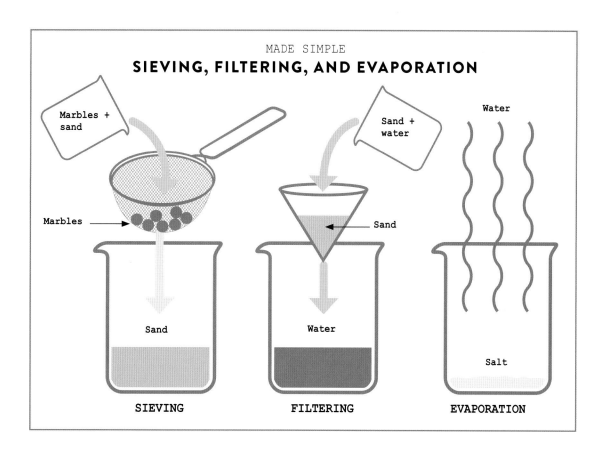

MADE SIMPLE
SIEVING, FILTERING, AND EVAPORATION

Marbles + sand

Sand + water

Water

Marbles

Sand

Sand

Water

Salt

SIEVING　　　　**FILTERING**　　　　**EVAPORATION**

STATES AND CHANGES

1. Salt is a:

a. Gas

b. Liquid

c. Solid

d. Plasma

2. The particles in a gas are:

a. Far apart

b. Slow

c. Close together

d. Held in place

3. What is the equation for density?

a. Density = Volume × Mass

b. Density = Mass ÷ Pressure

c. Density = Mass ÷ Volume

d. Density = Volume × Pressure

4. Which of these has the lowest melting point?

a. Gold

b. Plastic

c. Glass

d. Water

5. Gases and liquids diffuse from _____ to _____ concentration.

a. Low to high

b. Big to small

c. High to low

d. Good to poor

6. Condensation occurs when a _____ cools.

a. Gas

b. Liquid

c. Molecule

d. Solid

7. Which of these conditions is not required for snow to sublimate?

a. Strong sunlight

b. High pressure

c. Strong winds

d. Low humidity

8. Evaporation of which liquid helps humans cool down?

a. Blood

b. Tears

c. Stomach acid

d. Sweat

9. Which of these methods could be used to separate a solution?

a. Evaporation

b. Sieving

c. Stirring

d. Filtering

10. Which of these is an example of deposition?

a. Snow

b. Frost

c. Rain

d. Hail

Answers on page 214

SIMPLE SUMMARY

Matter exists in many different forms, depending on the conditions it's under, but on Earth it's mostly found in three states: solid, liquid, and gas.

- The density of a substance or material is the amount of matter packed into a given space. The more dense, the heavier it feels for its size.

- Substances move from areas of high concentration to areas of low concentration through diffusion.

- Matter can be changed from liquid to solid and back again by freezing and melting.

- When a liquid reaches a certain temperature, its molecules gain enough energy to break the weak bonds between them and become a gas. This change is called boiling.

- Sometimes it's only the water at the surface of a liquid that turns into a gas. This is known as evaporation.

- When gas cools, it turns to liquid. This change of state is condensation.

- When a substance is put under a set of conditions that cause it to skip the liquid phase entirely, these changes are known as sublimation and deposition.

- Mixtures are created when two substances are combined but there's no chemical reaction between them.

- A substance that dissolves is called a solute, and the substance it dissolves in is called a solvent.

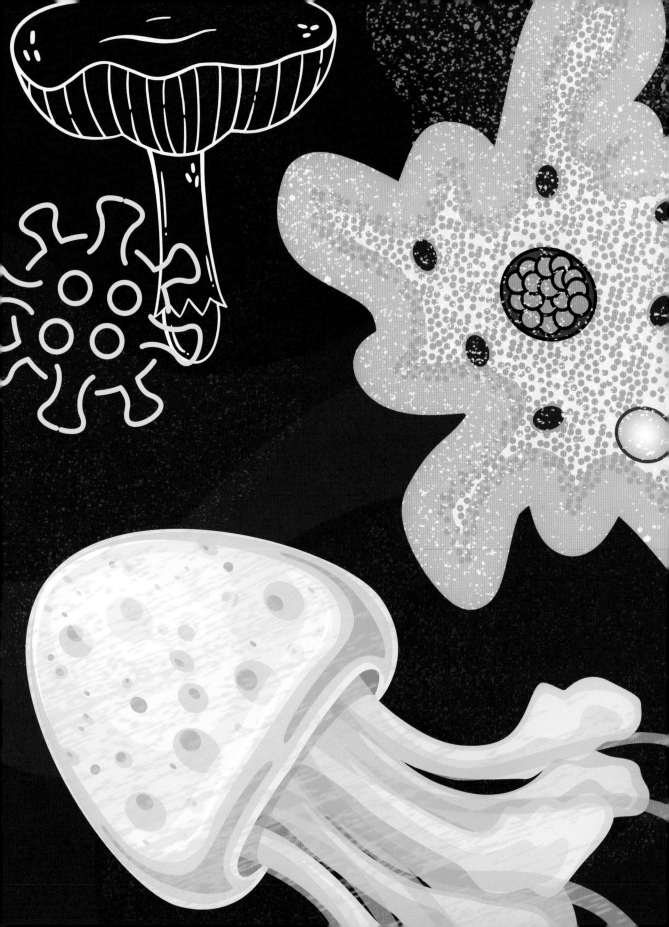

8

ORGANISMS AND ECOSYSTEMS

Life comes in all shapes and sizes. Tiny cells group together to make living things, and living things group together and interact in habitats and ecosystems. Don't be fooled by how peaceful a habitat may look—there's a new drama unfolding every second of the day.

WHAT YOU WILL LEARN

Building blocks of life

Organizing organisms

Microorganisms

Plants

Animals

Habitats and ecosystems

Earth's biomes

Biodiversity

Food chains and webs

LESSON 8.1

BUILDING BLOCKS OF LIFE

Everything alive is made up of cells. Some creatures are single cells, while humans are built from over 30 trillion. Most of these tiny building blocks are so small they can only be seen through a microscope, but they each have a hugely important job to do.

Inside each cell are components that work together to perform a particular role for a living thing. Among them are the nucleus, which contains a set of instructions and controls the other structures, and mitochondria that provide the cell with energy. These sit in a jellylike substance called cytoplasm, all wrapped up in a cell membrane that keeps the other components together and controls what can enter and leave the cell.

Plant cells have some extra structures because of the way they grow and get their energy. Around the cell membrane is a tougher cell wall that gives the cell strength and support. In the middle of the cytoplasm is the vacuole, a space filled with a sticky liquid called sap. Little blobs called chloroplasts

FACT

Cells called stem cells don't have a job when first created. They can split in half over and over to create new copies of themselves, and they have the potential to turn into many different types of cell. When an organism is growing or repairing, they become whichever cells the body needs more of.

PLANT CELL

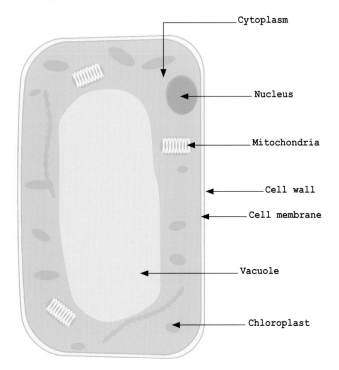

- Cytoplasm
- Nucleus
- Mitochondria
- Cell wall
- Cell membrane
- Vacuole
- Chloroplast

ANIMAL CELL

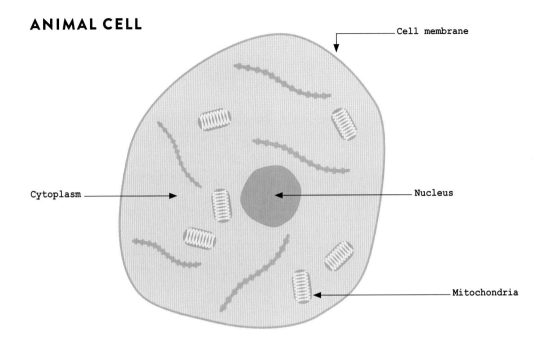

Cell membrane

Cytoplasm

Nucleus

Mitochondria

contain chlorophyll, a substance that gives leaves their green color and plays an important role in photosynthesis (see page 157).

Building a body

The instructions in the nucleus tell a cell whether it's a skin cell, a blood cell, or one of the hundreds of other cell types. Cells with the same job group together to form tissues such as muscles and connective tissue. Different tissues can then join forces to build organs such as the heart and the brain. Together all these cells make up a living thing, called an organism. Organs and tissues can be combined and arranged in all sorts of ways; that's why humans, pigeons, and jellyfish look so different, even though they're made from the same basic parts.

Cells are so small that they usually don't live very long. Old cells die off, but as soon as they do, younger cells split themselves in half to make new ones. This all happens very quickly; inside your body, millions of cells are replaced every single second.

ANSWER THIS

1. Which components are only found in plant cells?

2. Where are a cell's instructions found?

3. How many cells are in a human body?

4. Which cells can turn into other cell types?

LESSON 8.2

ORGANIZING ORGANISMS

Every living thing is different, but some organisms have more in common than others. Organisms that are very alike and can reproduce with one another are said to belong to the same species; humans, tigers, and great white sharks are examples of different species. All the world's species can be arranged into a huge family tree showing how they are related and how similar they are.

When scientists find a new species, they give it a name and try to work out which other organisms it is most like. By thinking about things like what it looks like, where it lives, what it eats, how it behaves, and what its DNA (see page 172) looks like, they decide which group to put it in. This naming and grouping is called taxonomy.

MADE SIMPLE
THE FIVE KINGDOMS

There are many ways to organize all the living things we have discovered, but the five kingdoms are the groups most people use. These groups are:

ANIMALS
Organisms that move around and get energy by eating

PLANTS
Organisms that get their energy from the Sun and usually don't move

FUNGI
Molds, mushrooms, toadstools, and yeast

PROTISTS
Single-cell organisms like amoebas

MONERA
The simplest single-cell organisms, including bacteria

 FACT So that experts around the world know they are talking about the same thing, every new species is given a Latin name: the first part tells you its genus (group); the second part is its unique species name.

LINNAEAN CLASSIFICATION

A Swedish scientist called Carl Linnaeus, who lived in the 1700s, invented a system for grouping, or "classifying," different organisms that is still used today.

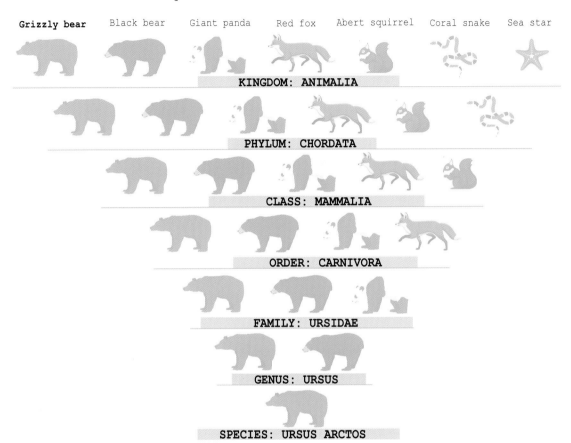

Grizzly bear Black bear Giant panda Red fox Abert squirrel Coral snake Sea star

KINGDOM: ANIMALIA

PHYLUM: CHORDATA

CLASS: MAMMALIA

ORDER: CARNIVORA

FAMILY: URSIDAE

GENUS: URSUS

SPECIES: URSUS ARCTOS

Within each of these groups are lots of smaller groups—it's like grouping together all the people in a huge family, then those that live in the same city, and then just the ones who live in the same house. Originally, scientists and explorers could only use things like an organism's appearance to decide which group it belonged to. Since technology like microscopes were invented, they've been able to study new discoveries in more detail, and sometimes species are moved from one group to another because it turns out they hadn't actually been put with their closest relatives.

ANSWER THIS

1. What's the name for a group of similar organisms that can reproduce?

2. What is taxonomy?

3. Why are organisms given Latin names?

LESSON
8.3 MICROORGANISMS

Some organisms are so small we can't see them without special equipment—these are the microorganisms. There are billions of them in the world, living everywhere from the soil to your unwashed socks. A few microorganisms like viruses and harmful bacteria can make us ill, but many species are very useful.

It's hard to imagine something so small you can't see it, but you can think about it like this: microorganisms (also known as microbes) are so tiny that hundreds of them would be able to fit on a full stop. They do lots of important jobs, such as breaking down plants and animals after they've died, turning milk into yogurt, and keeping the soil full of nutrients for plants to use.

TYPES OF MICROORGANISM

There are five types of microorganism:

 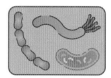  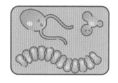 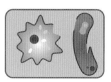

Bacteria are single-celled organisms without a nucleus. They can be shaped like balls, spirals, or rods.

Viruses are strange microbes that can only survive and multiply inside other living things. They pass from organism to organism, and cause illnesses like flu and chicken pox.

Microalgae, as with plants, make their own food through photosynthesis (see page 157). They like to live on water, and produce lots of the oxygen we breathe.

Microscopic fungi can be made of multiple cells or just one. Some cause diseases in plants, but others work to keep the soil healthy.

Protists are single-celled organisms that don't fit into any other groups because they are not animals, plants, fungi, or bacteria.

FACT Yeast is a microscopic fungus that people use to make bread. Yeast feeds on the sugar in flour and produces carbon dioxide gas as its waste. This gas fills the bread mix with hundreds of air bubbles, helping it rise in the oven and giving it a fluffy texture.

Germs

Harmful microorganisms are known as germs. Germs are the reason you have to wash and dry your hands before you eat and after you've been to the toilet. If they pass from your hands to your food, germs can end up inside your body. They reproduce very quickly in the warmth of your insides and can make you really unwell. Your body has lots of ways of protecting you from germs, but keeping your body and the things around you clean means there's less chance any bad microbes will harm you.

MADE SIMPLE
LIFE CYCLE OF A VIRUS

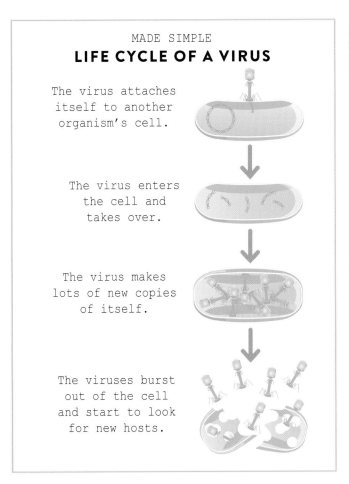

The virus attaches itself to another organism's cell.

The virus enters the cell and takes over.

The virus makes lots of new copies of itself.

The viruses burst out of the cell and start to look for new hosts.

ANSWER THIS

1. Which type of microbe can cause chicken pox?

2. Why is it important to wash your hands properly?

3. Where does a virus reproduce?

4. Which helpful microorganism is used in bread making?

LESSON
8.4 PLANTS

There are almost 400,000 species of plant, ranging from delicate daisies to enormous oak trees. Plants can't move around like animals can, but don't be fooled into thinking they don't do much—they're always growing and changing, and there are some amazing things going on in the inside.

Plants can be divided into two groups: flowering and nonflowering. Flowering plants grow flowers made of petals, and they include sunflowers, roses, and apple trees. Nonflowering plants such as pine trees, ferns, and moss never grow flowers or fruit.

FACT

While they can't get up and move from their spot in the soil, plants aren't completely still. They need the Sun's rays to fall on their leaves to stay alive, so many species grow toward sunlight. Plant some seeds and put the tray on a windowsill, and when shoots start to grow you'll see that they bend toward the window.

PARTS OF A FLOWERING PLANT

Flowers attract insects that help the plant make seeds.

Fruit holds seeds while they grow, then they drop to the ground or get eaten.

Leaves absorb sunlight and provide energy for the whole plant.

Stems support the plant, and transport water and nutrients to the other parts.

Roots take up water and nutrients (substances an organism can use as fuel) from the soil.

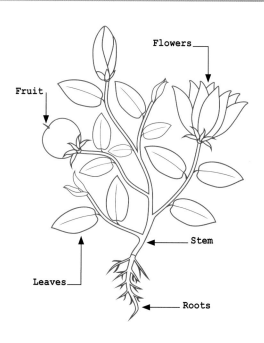

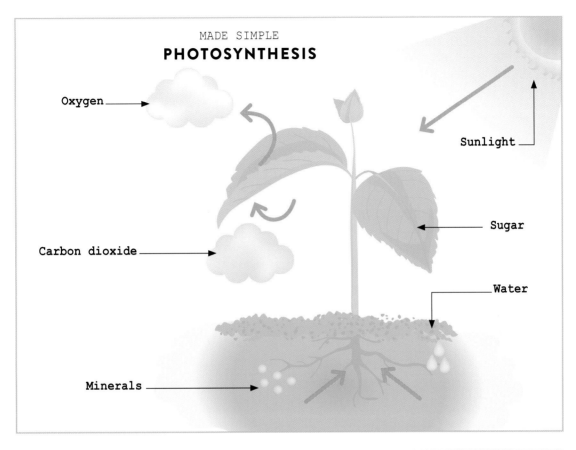

PHOTOSYNTHESIS

Oxygen

Sunlight

Carbon dioxide

Sugar

Water

Minerals

How plants get energy

Plants have an amazing way of getting the energy they need to grow—they use sunlight, water, and carbon dioxide (an invisible gas) to make sugar. The process is called photosynthesis ("photo" comes from the Greek word for light, and "synthesis" means making or putting things together), and it takes place inside a plant's leaves.

Carbon dioxide from the air enters the leaves through small holes called stomata. Water is sucked up from the soil by the plant's roots and then sent up thin tubes to the leaves. The green chlorophyll in the leaf cells (see page 151) absorbs sunlight as it hits the leaves, and the energy from the sunlight changes the water and carbon dioxide into a type of sugar called glucose. The reaction also creates oxygen, but plants don't need this gas so it escapes through the stomata into the air, where animals like us breathe it in (see page 194).

ANSWER THIS

1. How many species of plants are there?

2. Which three things do plants need for photosynthesis?

3. How does carbon dioxide get into a plant's leaves?

4. Why is photosynthesis important for humans?

8.5 ANIMALS

We've seen that animals are organisms that move around and have to eat to survive, but besides this, some species don't look like they have much in common. There are animals that can live underwater and animals that can fly through the air. With so much variation, how do we organize all the animals?

The two main groups of animals are the vertebrates and the invertebrates. Vertebrates are animals with spines, while invertebrates are those that don't have a backbone. Based on features they share, vertebrates can be divided into five smaller groups: fish, reptiles, amphibians, birds, and mammals. About 97 percent of all animals are invertebrates—most of these are insects, but the group also includes creatures like snails, spiders, worms, crabs, jellyfish, corals, and squid. Invertebrates like slugs and worms are soft, but others like lobsters and beetles protect themselves by growing hard cases called exoskeletons.

VERTEBRATES

Mammals
e.g., humans, whales, bears

Birds
e.g., kingfishers, robins, eagles

Fish
e.g., sharks, manta rays, salmon

Reptiles
e.g., alligators, tortoises, Komodo dragons

Amphibians
e.g., poison dart frogs, axolotls, newts

ANSWER THIS

1. What is the difference between a vertebrate and an invertebrate?

2. What percentage of animals are invertebrates?

3. What does cold-blooded mean?

4. Which vertebrate group do whales belong to?

INVERTEBRATES

Protozoa
Microscopic
single-celled
animals

Flatworms
Simple worms,
e.g., tapeworms

Echinoderms
Spiny animals
that live in
the ocean,
e.g., starfish,
sea urchins

Mollusks
Soft animals
often protected
by shells,
e.g., snails,
oysters

Annelids
Worms with
segmented bodies,
e.g., earthworms

Coelenterates
Soft animals that
live underwater;
some have stinging
cells, e.g.,
jellyfish

Arthropods
Animals with
exoskeletons and
jointed limbs

Myriapods
Long animals
with segmented
bodies and lots
of legs,
e.g.,
centipedes,
millipedes

Insects
Invertebrates
with six legs,
three body
sections, and
antennae,
e.g., ladybugs,
butterflies

Arachnids
Invertebrates
with eight legs
and two body
sections,
e.g., spiders,
scorpions

Crustaceans
Very diverse
group of
invertebrates,
e.g., crabs,
shrimp,
wood lice

8.6

HABITATS AND ECOSYSTEMS

Polar bears live on the ice, frogs live in ponds, and camels live in the desert. These are their habitats—the places in which they live in the wild. Some habitats are enormous, and the animals living in them can roam over many miles, while others are small and isolated.

A species' habitat could be anything from a meadow or forest to a beach or the ocean. The habitat provides an organism with everything it needs, including food, a home, and the chance to reproduce. Each species is adapted to its habitat and probably wouldn't survive in a different environment; a camel would be very cold and hungry at the North Pole and a polar bear would overheat in the desert.

Microhabitats

Even within a habitat there can be areas where conditions are very different. Think about a forest: the top branches of a tree get lots of sunshine and wind, but the patch of soil underneath a log is damp and dark. These places are called microhabitats, and they're the perfect homes for some of the organisms found in the larger habitat.

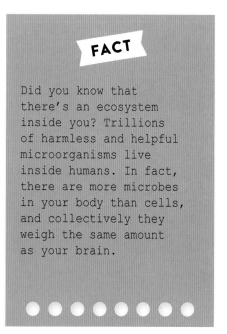

FACT

Did you know that there's an ecosystem inside you? Trillions of harmless and helpful microorganisms live inside humans. In fact, there are more microbes in your body than cells, and collectively they weigh the same amount as your brain.

Ecosystems

Organisms are never alone—they share their habitat with relatives and members of other species. The organisms living in the habitat interact with one another and with the nonliving (or "abiotic") parts of their environment, such as the soil, water, and rocks, forming a complicated community called an ecosystem. An ecosystem is always busy, full of organisms eating one another, helping one another, fighting over homes, and raising families.

AN ECOSYSTEM

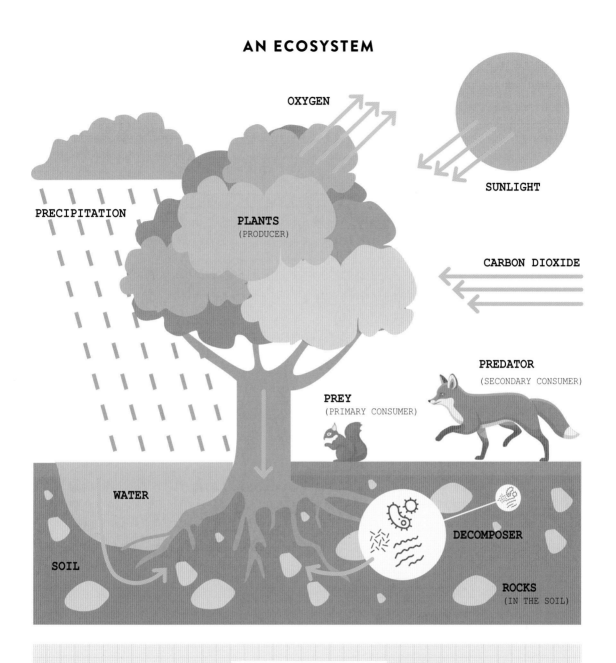

OXYGEN

SUNLIGHT

PRECIPITATION

PLANTS
(PRODUCER)

CARBON DIOXIDE

PREDATOR
(SECONDARY CONSUMER)

PREY
(PRIMARY CONSUMER)

WATER

DECOMPOSER

SOIL

ROCKS
(IN THE SOIL)

ANSWER THIS

1. What does a habitat provide the organisms that live there?

2. What is the name for a small habitat inside a larger habitat?

3. Which word is used to describe the nonliving parts of an ecosystem?

LESSON
8.7 EARTH'S BIOMES

From thick ice to burning sand, conditions change as you travel around the globe. Habitats are part of much larger communities of organisms that like to live in the same types of conditions, known as biomes. Together the biomes make up the biosphere, the layer of Earth where life exists.

Different areas of Earth experience different temperatures and weather conditions, and so are home to different plant and animal species. Places with similar conditions and wildlife can be grouped into biomes. There are six main biomes on land—tundra, taiga/boreal forest, temperate forest, tropical rainforest, savanna, and desert.

FACT

After the North and South Poles, the driest place in the world is the Atacama Desert in South America. Two large mountain ranges stop moisture from reaching the desert, so on average it receives less than 0.4 inches (1 centimeter) of rain in a year.

ANSWER THIS

1. What is the biosphere?

2. Which is the coldest biome?

3. Where are tropical rainforests found?

4. How many seasons are there on the savanna?

5. Which biome is the United States part of?

Watery biomes

The world's aquatic regions (areas covered in or near water) can be divided into biomes too, based on factors like how salty the water is and what lives there. The main aquatic biomes are:

Ponds and lakes: Pools of water completely surrounded by land.
Rivers and streams: Stretches of fresh water flowing through the land, usually to the sea.
Wetlands: Swampy areas where the land is covered in a layer of water but plants continue to grow.
Oceans: Large bodies of deep, salty water home to a huge variety of plants and animals.
Coral reefs: Reefs made of twisting coral, usually found in warm shallow water.
Estuaries: Where the fresh water of a river meets the salty sea, creating a unique ecosystem.

WHERE IN THE WORLD?

TUNDRA
The coldest of all the biomes and as dry as the desert. Almost nothing can grow in the freezing conditions, but animals like Arctic foxes have learned to survive here.

TAIGA/BOREAL FOREST
Cold and dry. Tall evergreen trees are the most common plants here, and animal residents include wolves, bears, and hawks.

SAVANNA
There are two long seasons—rainy and dry. Shrubs, grasses, and a few tall trees feed grazing animals like zebras and giraffes.

KEY Tundra · Taiga/boreal forest · Savanna · Desert · Temperate forest · Tropical rainforest · Mountainous · Chaparral/scrubland

DESERT
Hardly any rain falls, and only tough plants like cacti can grow here. Most of the animal inhabitants come out at night when it's cooler.

TEMPERATE FOREST
It never gets extremely hot or cold. Different plants and animals arrive with each of the seasons, and many of the trees lose their leaves in winter.

TROPICAL RAINFOREST
Wet and hot, and home to half of the planet's plant and animal species. Found close to the Equator.

BIODIVERSITY

Biodiversity—a word made by squashing "biological" and "diversity" together—is a term used to describe the variety of plants, animals, and other organisms within an area. Some places are rich with life, while others are home to just a few species. Biodiversity changes as conditions change, and it's now under threat from human activity.

Count up all the different species in an area and you have its biodiversity. The more diverse a region or habitat, the healthier and stronger it is. If a natural disaster or big environmental change occurs, there's a higher chance that some organisms will be able to survive and eventually recover. Organisms in an ecosystem interact and rely on one another for food, shelter, and building materials though, so if one species starts to decline it affects all the others.

While species such as red foxes and cats live in many places, some can only be found on a single island or in one particular forest. Areas that are home to lots of these unique residents but are under threat from humans are known as biodiversity hot spots—there are currently 36, and between them they contain almost 60 percent of the world's plant, mammal, reptile, bird, and amphibian species.

Benefits and threats
We benefit from the vast diversity of life on Earth. Not only is nature beautiful and enjoyable to look at, it also provides us with useful resources.

THE THREATS

DEFORESTATION   ANIMAL GRAZING   POLLUTION   CLIMATE CHANGE

No one knows how many species live on Earth because there are many we haven't discovered. Some scientists think there could be as many as a trillion, but most agree it's probably around 8.7 million. The majority are microorganisms invisible to the eye.

"Endemic species" are found only in one place. As Madagascar has been cut off from the rest of Africa for millions of years, thousands of unique plants and animals have evolved there and spread no further than the coast. Over 80 percent of the island's trees are endemic, as are most of its animal species.

Plants can be used to build shelters, make paper, and create furniture, and certain species can be turned into medicines.

Sadly, biodiversity is declining across the planet. Species have become extinct (see page 184) for many reasons since life began, but they're now vanishing at an alarming rate, mainly due to human activities like hunting and cutting down trees. If a species loses its home, its food source, or too many of its members, its survival becomes impossible and the biodiversity of the ecosystem falls.

ANSWER THIS

1. How many species do scientists think there are on Earth?

2. What is the main reason for the current decline in biodiversity?

3. How many biodiversity hot spots are there?

4. What percentage of Madagascar's trees are endemic?

DEVELOPMENT

HUNTING AND POACHING

ANIMAL TRADE

OVERFISHING

FOOD CHAINS AND WEBS

All living things need energy to grow, move, and stay healthy. Plants make energy from sunlight through photosynthesis (see page 157), but animals can't photosynthesize, and have to eat other organisms for energy. Energy passes from animal to animal in a food chain, and these chains can link together to form complex webs.

All food chains begin with a producer, an organism—usually a green plant—that makes its own food from the Sun and the nutrients in the ground. When the plant gets eaten, the energy it made is transferred into the animal's body. This first animal is known as the primary consumer, because it is the first organism in the chain to eat anything. The primary consumer is then eaten by a secondary consumer, and its energy goes to this new animal. Because the secondary consumer is eating another animal, it's known as a predator, and the primary consumer is its prey.

There can be any number of links in the chain, but eventually the apex predator comes along. This consumer hunts other animals but nothing in the habitat is big or brave enough to eat it while it's alive, so the species is said to be at the top of the food chain. The transfer of energy doesn't stop there though; when the apex predator dies, its body is eaten by scavengers or broken down by tiny organisms known as decomposers. Some of the energy and nutrients from the decomposed animal enter the soil where they can be used by plants, and the cycle starts all over again.

FACT

Animals can be put into different groups based on what they eat. Species that eat only plants are called herbivores, while those that stick to meat are carnivores. Creatures that, like humans, are equally happy eating plants and other animals are known as omnivores.

Forming webs

Just like us, most animals eat more than one type of food, so food chains can overlap and link together. Producers are almost always just producers (with the exception of a few plants that catch and digest animals), but animals can occupy several different positions in a food web. If a bird eats a berry and then eats a caterpillar munching on a leaf, it's both a primary consumer and a secondary consumer.

FOOD CHAIN

ANSWER THIS

1. What is at the start of every food chain?

2. What is another name for the predator at the top of the food chain?

3. Which word describes animals that only eat plants?

4. What is an omnivore?

5. What task do decomposers perform?

WOLF
Tertiary consumer and apex predator

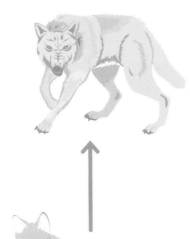

FOX
Secondary consumer

RODENT
Primary consumer

PLANT
Producer

ORGANISMS AND ECOSYSTEMS

1. **Roughly how many cells are in the human body?**
   a. 100,000
   b. 2 billion
   c. 30 trillion
   d. 40 million

2. **Which three things does a plant need for photosynthesis?**
   a. Sugar, sunlight, and carbon dioxide
   b. Carbon dioxide, water, and sunlight
   c. Water, oxygen, and carbon dioxide
   d. Sunlight, oxygen, and water

3. **All organisms are given scientific names in which language?**
   a. French
   b. English
   c. Greek
   d. Latin

4. **All the microbes in your body together weigh as much as which organ?**
   a. Brain
   b. Heart
   c. Lungs
   d. Liver

5. **Which of these is a microhabitat?**
   a. Meadow
   b. Lake
   c. Pile of leaves
   d. Garden

6. **Lions, sheep, and horses belong to which animal group?**
   a. Mammals
   b. Echinoderms
   c. Mollusks
   d. Amphibians

7. **Which of these is not one of Earth's biomes?**
   a. Savanna
   b. Taiga
   c. Antarctica
   d. Tundra

8. **Which name is given to an animal that only eats meat?**
   a. Herbivore
   b. Omnivore
   c. Decomposer
   d. Carnivore

9. **Biodiversity hot spots contain what percentage of the world's plants and animals?**
   a. Nearly 90 percent
   b. Nearly 40 percent
   c. 100 percent
   d. Nearly 60 percent

10. **Which microorganism can only survive in other organisms' cells?**
    a. Virus
    b. Bacteria
    c. Fungus
    d. Protist

Answers on page 215

SIMPLE SUMMARY

Tiny cells group together to make living things, and living things group together and interact in habitats and ecosystems.

- Everything alive is made up of cells. Some creatures are single cells, while humans are built from over 30 trillion of them. Cells with the same job group together to form tissues such as muscles and connective tissue.

- All living things are grouped into one of the five kingdoms: animals, plants, fungi, protists, monera.

- Microorganisms do lots of important jobs, and can be classified into bacteria, viruses, microalgae, microscopic fungi, or protists.

- Plants use sunlight, water, and carbon dioxide to make sugar—a process called photosynthesis.

- The two main groups of animals are vertebrates (animals with spines) and invertebrates (without a backbone).

- A habitat provides an organism with everything it needs. Habitats are part of much larger communities of organisms that like to live in the same types of conditions, known as biomes.

- The nonliving parts of an organism's environment form an ecosystem.

- Biodiversity describes the variety of plants, animals, and other organisms within an area. Areas that are home to lots of unique species but are under threat from humans are known as biodiversity hot spots.

- Animals eat other organisms for energy. Energy passes from animal to animal in a food chain, and these chains can link together to form webs.

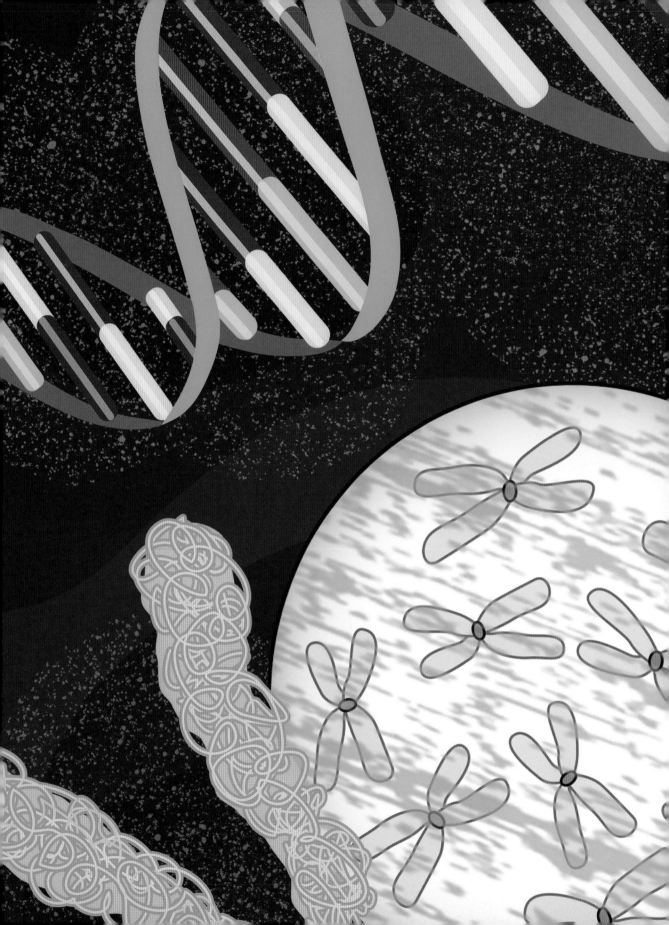

9

GENES AND EVOLUTION

Why do you look a bit like your relatives? Why are some people so much taller than others? And where did your pet dog come from? The answers to these questions and many more can be found in DNA, a twisted molecule that holds all the secrets of life.

WHAT YOU WILL LEARN

DNA	Competition
Inheritance	Selective breeding and domestication
Evolution	Extinction
Adaptation	Fossils

LESSON

9.1   DNA

Inside almost all of your cells is a nucleus containing genetic information—all the instructions needed to make your body and keep it running. The instructions are stored as code in long molecules called DNA. The code in every organism's DNA is unique, which is why there are so many different types of living things and why none of them looks exactly like you.

A single DNA molecule looks like a twisted ladder, a shape that's known as a double helix. All the DNA molecules in a nucleus are organized into bundles called chromosomes. Different species have different numbers of chromosomes; yellow fever mosquitoes have three pairs in each cell, the Atlas blue butterfly has up to 226 pairs, and humans have 23 pairs (46 in total). Of the pairs, 22 contain most of the information about what you look like and how your body works, while the 23rd pair determines your sex.

HOW DNA IS STORED

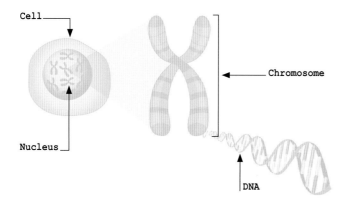

Cell

Nucleus

Chromosome

DNA

How does DNA work?
A strand of DNA is made up of a sequence of tiny units called nucleotides, each containing a sugar molecule, a molecule called a phosphate, and a "base." There are four different bases: adenine (A), cytosine (C), guanine (G), and thymine (T).

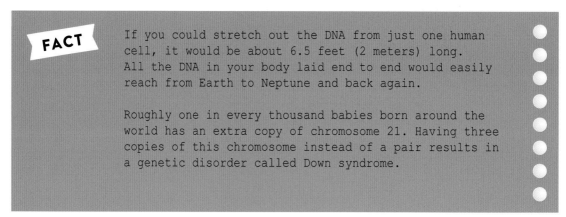

FACT

If you could stretch out the DNA from just one human cell, it would be about 6.5 feet (2 meters) long. All the DNA in your body laid end to end would easily reach from Earth to Neptune and back again.

Roughly one in every thousand babies born around the world has an extra copy of chromosome 21. Having three copies of this chromosome instead of a pair results in a genetic disorder called Down syndrome.

INSIDE A CHROMOSOME

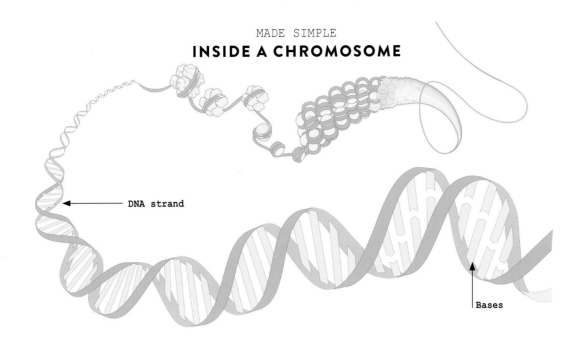

DNA strand

Bases

The base of one nucleotide pairs up with the base of another to form the ladder shape, and it's the order of these bases along the DNA chain that makes up your unique code. Special molecules in the cell read the sequence and use the information to make proteins and carry out other tasks.

Short sections of DNA that carry the information for a certain characteristic are known as genes. You have thousands of genes, carrying information about everything from the color of your hair to the length of your toes. Members of a species look similar but not the same because there are multiple versions of each gene, known as alleles. This creates differences between organisms, which scientists call genetic variation. For example, there are several alleles of the gene for eye color.

ANSWER THIS

1. What are the four different bases?

2. What shape is a strand of DNA?

3. What is the name for different forms of a gene?

4. How many pairs of chromosomes do humans have?

9.2 INHERITANCE

You've probably noticed that people tend to look like their relatives. It's true of other species too; from puppies to poppies, organisms usually look more like their parents and close family members than other individuals. This is because of inheritance— the passing down of genes from parent to offspring.

DNA is known as "hereditary material" because it can be passed from one generation to the next. While most human cells have a full set of DNA, sex cells have 23 single chromosomes—exactly half the code needed for a complete human. When a sperm cell meets an egg, the two cells combine their DNA to make a full set of instructions for a new person. The baby that develops from the cells inherits genes—and therefore certain characteristics—from each parent. You inherited half of your genes from each of your parents, which is why you might have a nose like your mother's and the same eye color as your father. Maybe you look more like one of your grandparents; because your parents got half their genes from each of their parents, you share a quarter of your DNA with each grandparent.

GENETIC INHERITANCE

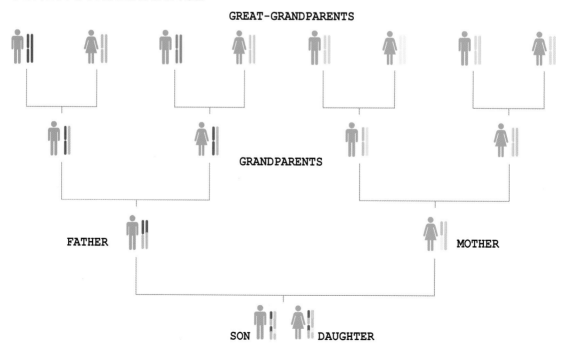

Some alleles are dominant over others. If you inherit a dominant allele from one parent and a recessive (nondominant) allele from the other, the body takes its instructions from the dominant allele. The allele for brown eyes is dominant over the blue eye allele. One brown eye allele and one blue result in brown eyes; people only have blue eyes if they received blue eye alleles from both parents.

As different pairs of people have babies together and DNA passes down through generations, genes are combined in new ways. Genes combine in a new way even when the same couple has a second baby; this is why siblings don't look the same unless they're identical twins. Identical twins look like each other because they come from a single fertilized egg (see page 207) that splits in half to form two separate bundles of cells with the same DNA.

Not all of your characteristics come from inherited genes—some can come from your lifestyle and surroundings. These are called environmental characteristics, and include things like piercings, suntan, scars, and the language you speak. They can't be passed on to future generations because they were caused by something outside the body and there are no instructions for them in the DNA.

EYE GENES

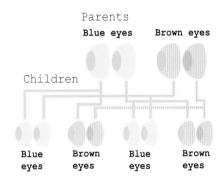

Parents
Blue eyes   **Brown eyes**

Children

Blue eyes   **Brown eyes**   **Blue eyes**   **Brown eyes**

Recessive blue eye allele

Dominant brown eye allele

MADE SIMPLE
INHERITED VS. ENVIRONMENTAL CHARACTERISTICS

INHERITED CHARACTERISTICS
• Natural hair color
• Eye color
• Ability to roll tongue
• Nose shape
• Cheek dimples

ENVIRONMENTAL CHARACTERISTICS
• Language
• Favorite song
• Piercings
• Scars

CHARACTERISTICS INFLUENCED BY BOTH GENES AND ENVIRONMENT
• Height • Weight
• Reading ability
• Strength
• Personality

9.3 EVOLUTION

If you had a time machine and went back a few million years, there would be plants and animals that no longer exist (see page 185), and you might not recognize some of the species that are still around today. Species change over time, developing new characteristics that help them to survive.

Charles Darwin was an English naturalist (an expert in nature) who became famous for his theory of evolution. When he was 22, Darwin joined a voyage on a ship called the HMS *Beagle*. As he explored the world, he noticed that living things were always competing with each other to stay alive. Darwin realized that small differences between individuals in a species caused by genetic variation meant that some were more likely to survive—a tortoise with a longer neck could reach higher leaves, for example, and a plant with bigger thorns was less likely to be eaten by animals.

Individuals that happen to have a combination of genes and traits helpful for survival are more likely to live long enough to reproduce and pass on useful genes to their offspring. Darwin called this idea "natural selection." Over time, natural selection causes characteristics that help a species survive in its habitat to become more common. Gradually, the appearance or behavior of the species changes—this is evolution.

For example, a population of rodents moves to an area with dark rocks. Due to genetic variation, some members of the group are black, while the others are white. White rodents are more easily spotted against the rock, so more are eaten by predators. The surviving rodents reproduce and pass on their genes. There are more black rodents in the next generation.

FACT — Chimpanzees and bonobos are our closest living relatives—we share about 99 percent of our DNA with an ancestor that lived around 7 million years ago. There were once other species of humans on Earth, but they all became extinct thousands or millions of years ago, so now our species, *Homo sapiens*, is the only type of human left alive.

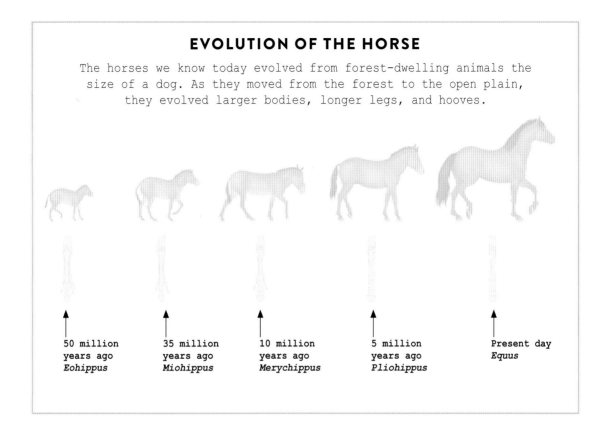

EVOLUTION OF THE HORSE

The horses we know today evolved from forest-dwelling animals the size of a dog. As they moved from the forest to the open plain, they evolved larger bodies, longer legs, and hooves.

50 million years ago
Eohippus

35 million years ago
Miohippus

10 million years ago
Merychippus

5 million years ago
Pliohippus

Present day
Equus

Close relations

It's because of evolution that there are so many species on Earth. They're all related to some degree; humans are closely related to primates like chimpanzees and gorillas, but we also share an ancestor with everything from sharks to daffodils. We're all connected in a giant family tree that stretches all the way back to the first organisms, billions of years ago. The first living things all looked similar but, as they spread out and met new challenges, different genes became useful. Over many generations small changes took place, until eventually groups living in different habitats changed so much that they became new species.

ANSWER THIS

1. Who came up with the theory of evolution?

2. What does the idea of "natural selection" mean?

3. Small _____ between individuals mean some are more likely to survive.

4. Horses evolved _____ bodies and _____ legs.

5. Can an individual organism evolve?

9.4 ADAPTATION

Each species has a habitat, an area or type of environment it prefers to live in (see page 160). Habitats can vary from hot and dry to cold and wet, and each presents a different set of challenges for the plants and animals that live there.

Over time, species evolve features and characteristics that help them to survive in their particular habitat. These are called adaptations. There are three main types of adaptation:

1. Structural A change in the shape, structure, or appearance of the organism. Structural adaptations include a giraffe's long neck for reaching tall trees and a caterpillar's camouflage.

2. Behavioral A change in the way members of the species live or behave. Animals in hot climates are often nocturnal, waking up at night when it's cooler. Some predators live and hunt in packs so they can kill larger prey, while many prey species have evolved ways of warning each other that predators are nearby.

3. Physiological Physiology is the study of all the processes going on inside an organism. Physiological adaptations include things like a strong sense of smell, a change in diet, and the production of venom or poison.

FACT

Birds are adapted for a life of flying. They have powerful muscles in their chests to move their wings, and their bones are hollow so that their bodies are as light as possible.

Some species of butterfly, moth, and lizard have adapted to life in the forest by evolving camouflage that makes them look just like dead leaves. Against real leaves, they're almost invisible to hungry predators.

POLAR BEAR ADAPTATIONS

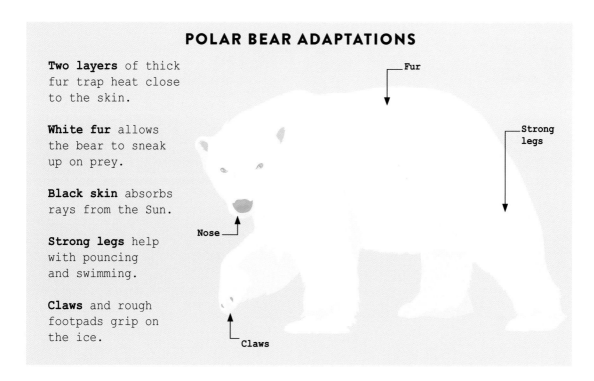

Two layers of thick fur trap heat close to the skin.

White fur allows the bear to sneak up on prey.

Black skin absorbs rays from the Sun.

Strong legs help with pouncing and swimming.

Claws and rough footpads grip on the ice.

Fur

Strong legs

Nose

Claws

Plant adaptations

Plants are adapted to their habitats just like animals. Some rainforest plants have cup-shaped leaves that collect water, and plants that grow underwater have soft leaves so they can move with the waves and not get broken.

Plants that live in arid (hot and dry) habitats are called xerophytes. They have several tactics for surviving with very little rain. These plants have long roots that wind through the ground in search of water. Some, like succulents, are round and fleshy with a waxy layer that keeps water in. Cacti have evolved thin spines instead of leaves—these spikes stop animals from eating them and reduce the amount of water lost through evapotranspiration (see page 83).

DRY DESERT PLANTS

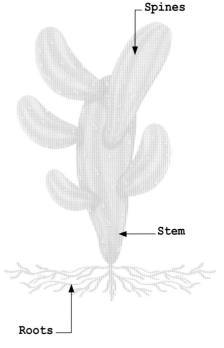

Leaves are reduced to spines to defend the plant and prevent water loss.

Thick stem stores a supply of water.

Network of long roots search for water in the ground.

Spines

Stem

Roots

9.5 COMPETITION

The natural world might look peaceful, but there's a battle going on around every corner. Habitats provide organisms with nutrients, mates, and homes, but there's often not enough to go around. Living things must compete with each other for important resources that will increase their chances of surviving and reproducing.

Competition can be either intraspecific or interspecific. Intraspecific competition is between members of the same species, like robins competing for territory, while interspecific competition occurs between members of different species. Examples of interspecific competition include hyenas and lions fighting over a zebra carcass and different plants competing for minerals and sunlight. Intraspecific competition is often fiercer because members of a species occupy the same niche (role in an ecosystem) and are always after the same resources.

FACT

In between competing with each other, animals can sometimes cooperate. Organisms from the same species or different species will help each other if cooperation means they both stand a better chance of survival. Some species of rainforest plant, for example, let ants live inside their stems—in exchange, the insects protect the plants from attackers.

Competition often leads to the evolution of new or exaggerated features. Bright feathers and enthusiastic dances help males of the same bird species compete over females, and the giant antlers of male deer are used in fights over mates and territory. When a new species moves into a habitat, the new competition can put pressure on the species already living there and slowly change the way they evolve.

Predator and prey

Predators and prey are locked in a constant fight because each species wants a different outcome; the predator wants to eat the prey, but the prey wants to avoid being eaten. Predators and prey evolve together because they have such a big impact on each other's survival. If a prey species evolves longer legs to run away faster, then the predator must evolve a faster run to keep up; and if a predator evolves better eyesight, its prey will only survive if it evolves better camouflage.

MADE SIMPLE
PREDATOR-PREY EVOLUTION

Predator and prey species affect
each other's evolution.

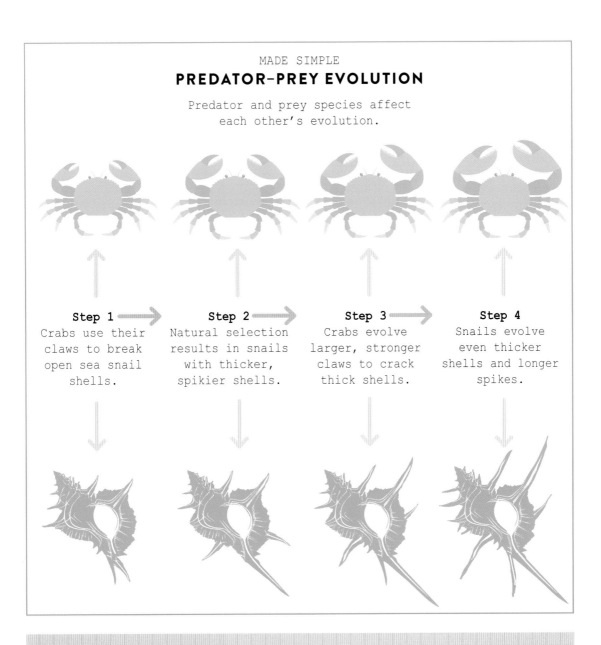

Step 1 ➡️
Crabs use their
claws to break
open sea snail
shells.

Step 2 ➡️
Natural selection
results in snails
with thicker,
spikier shells.

Step 3 ➡️
Crabs evolve
larger, stronger
claws to crack
thick shells.

Step 4
Snails evolve
even thicker
shells and longer
spikes.

⟩ ANSWER THIS ⟨

1. Male peacocks competing over a female is an example of _____ competition.

2. Which type of competition is usually the most fierce?

3. If they're both likely to benefit from it, organisms can _____.

4. Organisms compete over important _____.

LESSON
9.6

SELECTIVE BREEDING AND DOMESTICATION

Many people share their lives with pets and couldn't imagine being without them, but we haven't always had such a close relationship with animals. Our ancestors created the first bonds with these other species, and those bonds shaped how our animal companions have evolved.

Natural selection happens because of pressures in an organism's natural environment, but humans can influence how a species changes too. For thousands of years, people have been choosing to breed certain individuals to create plants and animals with useful characteristics. This is called selective breeding (or artificial selection), and it's the process that has created tall wheat, dairy cows that produce a lot of milk, new varieties of flowering plant, and hundreds of different dog breeds.

FACT

There are over 300 breeds of domestic dog. They all belong to the same species, *Canis familiaris*, but have been selectively bred over thousands of years to produce breeds ranging from tiny Chihuahuas to Great Danes. Different breeds were created for different jobs, like hunting, fighting, guarding, herding, and keeping people company.

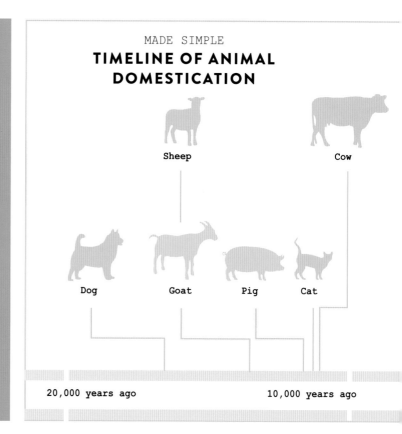

MADE SIMPLE
TIMELINE OF ANIMAL DOMESTICATION

Sheep

Cow

Dog

Goat

Pig

Cat

20,000 years ago   10,000 years ago

Food and friendship

Animal and plant species that have been kept by humans for many generations are said to be "domesticated." For thousands of years, people have been catching or taming wild animals and selectively breeding the ones with the friendliest natures and most useful traits. Dogs are our oldest companions, having lived alongside humans for at least 20,000 years. Descended from wild gray wolves, dogs gave humans fur and protection and could be used to pull sleds.

As humans began to farm and store food instead of relying entirely on hunting and gathering, they domesticated livestock like goats, sheep, chickens, pigs, and cows. Later, domesticated donkeys, horses, and camels provided people with transport and a way of moving heavy things. Animals that live in groups in the wild are easiest to domesticate because they're used to following a leader. Cats are unusual because their wild ancestors were used to living alone before they started spending time with humans. Some scientists believe cats are only partly domesticated, because they're still very independent and have changed less in appearance and behavior than other domestic species.

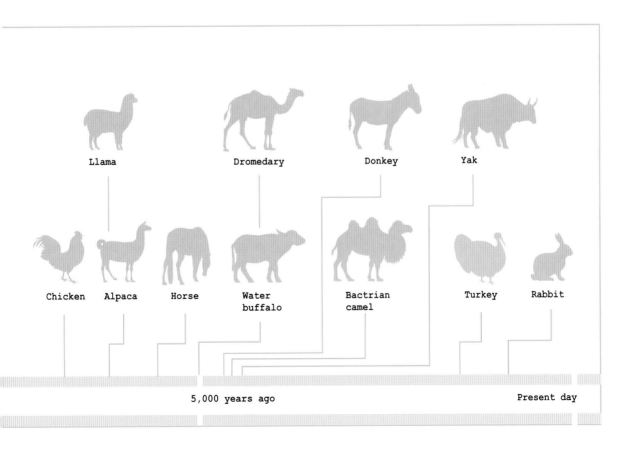

LESSON
9.7 EXTINCTION

Just like an individual organism can be killed, whole species can die too. If an illness, natural disaster, or other threat such as hunting means that every last member of a species dies, the species is said to be extinct.

Evolution happens very slowly, so sudden changes to the environment can leave a species unable to compete for resources or survive. Changes that can put a species at risk of extinction include habitat loss, a new disease, a new predator or competitor in the area, competition with humans, and physical changes to the habitat like drought. Extinct species are lost forever, because there are no individuals left to reproduce and pass on genes to a new generation.

A species that's at risk of going extinct is said to be endangered. Thousands of species are currently considered to be endangered, including giant pandas, tigers, and African penguins, and the population size of thousands of other species is still unknown. The smaller a population gets, the less genetic variation there is in

MASS EXTINCTIONS

Number of groups of organisms alive on Earth (thousands)

▼ Mass extinction events

Millions of years ago

FACT Some people believe that in the future, scientists will be able to bring back extinct species like the dodo and even the dinosaurs using new cloning techniques from fossilized DNA.

Sometimes a species is thought to be extinct for many years before reappearing. No one had seen Wallace's giant bee, the largest species of bee in the world, since 1981, until it was rediscovered in an Indonesian forest in January 2019.

MASS EXTINCTION EVENTS

1 ORDIVICIAN-SILURIAN
- 440 million years ago
- 86% of species lost

2 LATE DEVONIAN
- 365 million years ago
- 75% of species lost

3 PERMIAN-TRIASSIC
- 252 million years ago
- 96% of species lost

4 TRIASSIC-JURASSIC
- 201 million years ago
- 80% of species lost

5 CRETACEOUS-PALEOGENE
- 66 million years ago
- 75% of species lost

6 HOLOCENE
- 11,700 years ago to present day

the species. Less variation means that the species is less likely to be able to adapt to future changes, so endangered organisms can become extinct very quickly if conditions change in their habitat. Endangered species are also at risk from hunters and collectors, because "rare" plants and animals can often be sold for lots of money at illegal markets.

Mass extinction

Sometimes many species go extinct at once. This is called mass extinction. Around three-quarters of all the plant and animal species on Earth, including the dinosaurs, went extinct 66 million years ago in the Cretaceous-Paleogene extinction event (or K-Pg event, for short). The cause isn't known for sure, but the most popular theory is that a large asteroid hit the Earth and the impact set off natural disasters and sent up huge clouds of dust that blocked out the Sun.

LESSON

9.8 FOSSILS

Even though they became extinct long before humans evolved, we know lots about species like the ammonite and the triceratops. Some of our knowledge about their appearance, lifestyle, and behavior comes from studying closely related species still alive today, but we know that they existed in the first place because of fossils.

FACT

Not all fossils are made from whole animals or plants. Paleontologists (scientists who study fossils) have found fossilized footprints, eggs, and even poop.

Sedimentary rock is created when small pieces of rock and other debris are squashed by water (see page 78). Millions of years ago, the bodies of dead plants and animals ended up among the sediment and eventually became part of the rock. Fossils preserve information about the organisms, giving us a glimpse into the past every time one is discovered.

ANSWER THIS

1. Which type of rock are fossils found in?

2. Which parts of an organism aren't fossilized?

3. What is the name for a scientist who studies fossils?

4. How are fossils brought to the surface?

5. Organisms that died at different times are found in different _____ of the rock.

HOW A FOSSIL IS FORMED

1 DEATH
An animal dies and sinks down to an ocean floor or riverbed.

2 DECAY
Soft parts like eyeballs and organs quickly rot away, but hard parts like bones, shells, and teeth remain.

3 COVERING
The remains are gradually covered by layers of sediment. The weight of all the sediment pushes down, and the remains of the animal become part of the sedimentary rock.

4 MOVEMENT
Movements in the Earth's crust bring the rock layer containing the fossil to the surface.

5 REVELATION
When the rock is weathered or broken open, the fossil is revealed.

GENES AND EVOLUTION

1. In total, how many chromosomes does a human have in each cell?

   a. 41
   b. 48
   c. 42
   d. 46

2. Which letters represent the four bases in DNA?

   a. A, B, C, D
   b. A, C, G, T
   c. A, D, P, T
   d. A, B, G, P

3. Which of these is not a behavioral adaptation?

   a. Being nocturnal—waking up at night when it's cool
   b. Hibernating—sleeping through cold weather
   c. Migrating—moving to a warmer place in winter
   d. Being furry—having thick hair for warmth

4. Evolution happens very _____

   a. Slowly
   b. Suddenly
   c. Quickly
   d. Rarely

5. Competition between members of the same species is known as...

   a. Interspecific competition
   b. Intragenic competition
   c. Intergalactic competition
   d. Intraspecific competition

6. Which species did domestic dogs evolve from?

   a. Brown hyena
   b. Gray wolf
   c. African wild dog
   d. Maned wolf

7. When was the extinction event that wiped out the dinosaurs?

   a. 66 million years ago
   b. 44 billion years ago
   c. 55 billion years ago
   d. 33 million years ago

8. Which part of an animal cannot be fossilized?

   a. Bone
   b. Tooth
   c. Eye
   d. Shell

9. What is the name for differences between the DNA of organisms?

   a. Genetic inheritance
   b. Natural selection
   c. Genetic variation
   d. Natural variety

10. The only people who share the same DNA are...

    a. Cousins
    b. Mothers and daughters
    c. Grandparents and grandchildren
    d. Identical twins

Answers on page 216

SIMPLE SUMMARY

Inside almost all of your cells is a nucleus containing genetic information, your DNA—all the instructions needed to make your body and keep it running.

• DNA is known as "hereditary material" because it can be passed from one generation to the next.

• Darwin's "natural selection" theory proposes that individuals with a combination of genes and traits helpful for survival are more likely to live long enough to reproduce and pass on useful genes to their offspring.

• Over time, species evolve features and characteristics, known as adaptations, that help them to survive in their particular habitat.

• Living things must compete with each other for important resources that will increase their chances of surviving and reproducing.

• Selective breeding (or artificial selection) occurs when people choose to breed certain individuals to create plants and animals with useful characteristics.

• Changes that can put a species at risk of extinction can include habitat loss, a new disease, a new predator or competitor in the area, competition with humans, and physical changes to the habitat such as drought.

• Millions of years ago, the bodies of dead plants and animals ended up among the sediment and eventually became part of the rock, as fossils.

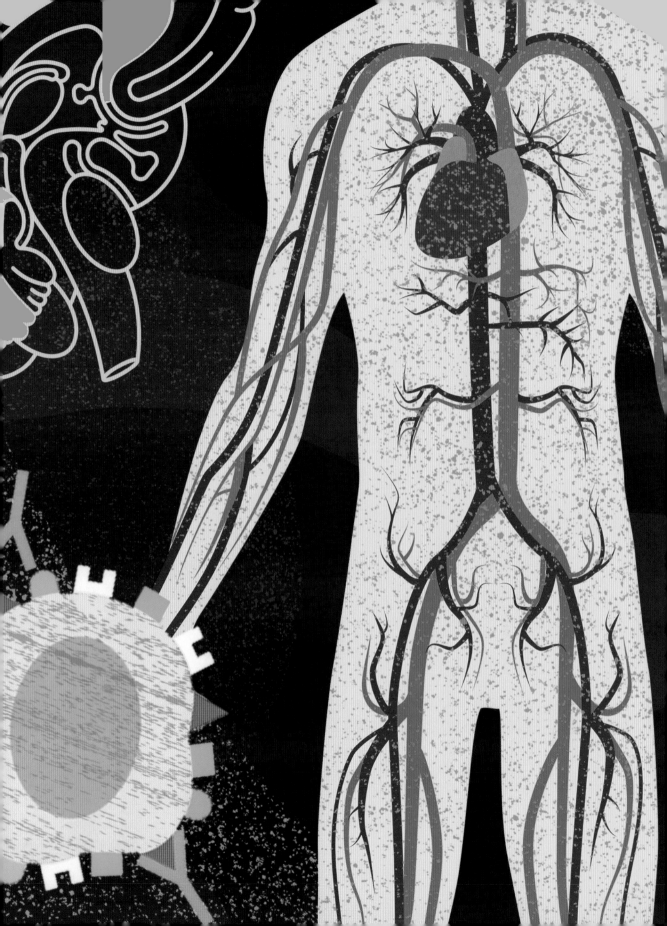

10

THE HUMAN BODY

Like a factory full of different machines, your body
is packed with organs and systems that each carry out
their own important tasks, day and night. Together they
give you energy, power your thoughts, help you move,
and keep you healthy.

WHAT YOU WILL LEARN

The skeleton and muscles

The respiratory system

The circulatory system

Inside the mouth

The digestive system

The immune system

The nervous system

The reproductive system

LESSON
10.1 THE SKELETON AND MUSCLES

Under your skin is a complex collection of tissues that work together to keep you alive. The skeleton supports it all, and the muscles allow you to move your body from one place to another.

MUSCULOSKELETAL SYSTEM

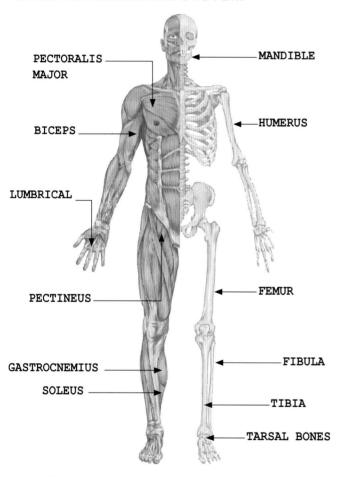

PECTORALIS MAJOR

BICEPS

LUMBRICAL

PECTINEUS

GASTROCNEMIUS

SOLEUS

MANDIBLE

HUMERUS

FEMUR

FIBULA

TIBIA

TARSAL BONES

The adult human skeleton is made up from 206 bones. A baby has about 300 bones when it's born, but over time some join together. Without a skeleton you'd be very floppy and moving around would be hard. The skeleton has four important jobs:

1. To support all the other parts of the body
2. To help the body to move
3. To protect soft organs like the brain, heart, and lungs
4. To make new blood cells (see page 196)

> **FACT**
>
> Skeletal muscle isn't the only type of muscle. Cardiac muscles make up the walls of the heart (see page 197), while smooth muscles can be found in the walls of several other organs. Altogether, your muscles make up almost half of your body weight.

JOINT

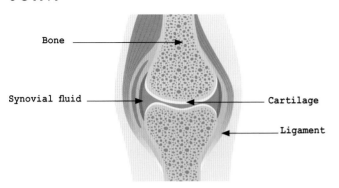

Bone

Synovial fluid

Cartilage

Ligament

Joints

Bones such as ribs are fused together and can't move much, but others like the leg bones and the jaw need to be able to move in different directions. These bones are linked together at points called joints. The end of each bone in a joint is covered with a smooth substance called cartilage and made slippery with a liquid called synovial fluid—these substances allow the bones to move past one another without rubbing and causing damage. Short pieces of tissue called ligaments hold the bones together and make sure they don't move apart.

Muscles

Skeletal muscles are soft tissues attached to the skeleton. There are more than 600 different skeletal muscles in the body, all helping the body to move. Muscles pull movable bones by getting shorter, or "contracting," but they can't push the bones back to where they were. So that you're not stuck forever with your knee bent or your arm above your head, muscles work in pairs— one contracts and pulls the bone one way, and its partner on the other side pulls it the other way.

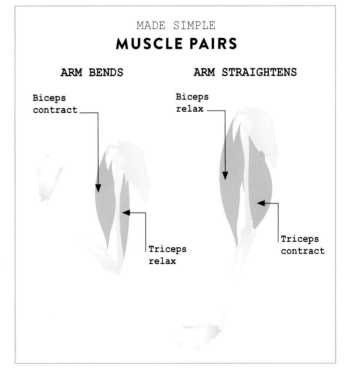

MADE SIMPLE
MUSCLE PAIRS

ARM BENDS

Biceps contract

Triceps relax

ARM STRAIGHTENS

Biceps relax

Triceps contract

LESSON
10.2 THE RESPIRATORY SYSTEM

Hold your breath for too long and you'll start to feel strange—this is because your cells are running out of energy and need more oxygen to keep working properly. The respiratory system takes oxygen from the air and delivers it to the whole body.

The respiratory system is a group of organs and tissues that supply all the cells in the body with the oxygen they need to turn food into energy for movement, growth, and repair. The process of using oxygen and glucose to create energy is called aerobic respiration.

INSIDE THE ALVEOLI

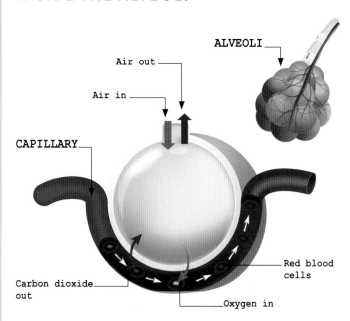

Into the lungs

Although it happens without you thinking about it, breathing is quite complex. Muscles around your middle pull down a sheet of muscle called the diaphragm. This movement gives the lungs room to expand and draw in air, which enters through the nose and mouth, and travels down the trachea, or windpipe. As air nears the lungs, the trachea splits into two passageways called

Labels: Air out, Air in, ALVEOLI, CAPILLARY, Carbon dioxide out, Oxygen in, Red blood cells

RESPIRATORY SYSTEM

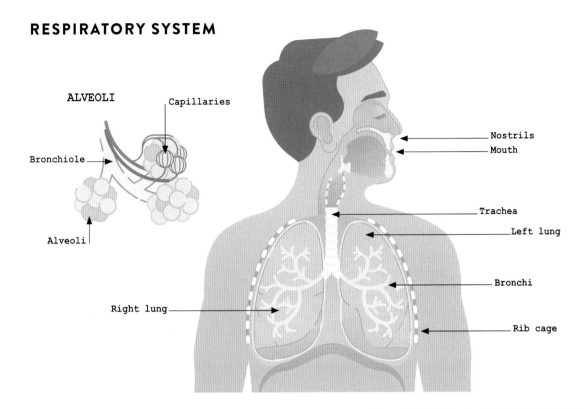

ALVEOLI

Capillaries

Bronchiole

Alveoli

Nostrils

Mouth

Trachea

Left lung

Bronchi

Right lung

Rib cage

bronchi. One bronchus goes to each lung, where it divides into smaller tubes called bronchioles. Every bronchiole ends in a bunch of lumpy air sacs called alveoli. There are millions of alveoli in each lung, together making up the surface area of a tennis court.

Gas exchange
Running across the surface of the alveoli are lots of tiny blood vessels called capillaries. As oxygen enters the lungs, it flows into the alveoli and diffuses through their thin walls into the blood. Red blood cells (see page 196) collect the oxygen and travel around the body, delivering it to cells so they can convert food into energy.

Carbon dioxide makes up part of the air and is a waste product of aerobic respiration. Our bodies can't use it, so it diffuses from the blood into the alveoli and leaves as we breathe out. Breathing out empties the lungs so they're ready to take in a new supply of oxygen.

(see page 196)

ANSWER THIS

1. Which two things are needed for aerobic respiration?

2. What type of cell carries oxygen around the body?

3. Which gas is a waste product of aerobic respiration?

4. Why can we only use anaerobic respiration for a short time?

5. What does aerobic respiration provide the body with?

THE CIRCULATORY SYSTEM

The circulatory system involves the movement of blood around the body in a network of tubes called blood vessels. Blood carries important supplies like water, nutrients, and oxygen to the cells and takes away any waste they produce.

The strong muscles of the heart pump the blood to keep it moving all the time. Blood is made up of red blood cells, white blood cells, and platelets. All three types of cell are made inside the bone marrow (the soft tissue inside large bones), but they play different parts in the system.

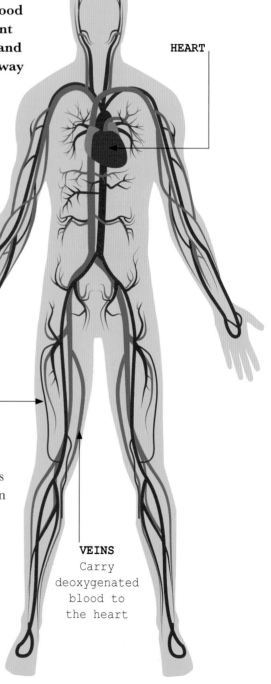

HEART

HUMAN CIRCULATORY SYSTEM

ARTERIES
Carry oxygenated blood away from the heart

VEINS
Carry deoxygenated blood to the heart

- **Red blood cells** have small dents on their surface for holding oxygen and carrying it around the body.
- **White blood cells** patrol the body, fighting off any harmful microorganisms that get in (see page 202).
- **Platelets** are tiny blood cells that form clots and scabs to stop wounds from bleeding.

HE HEART

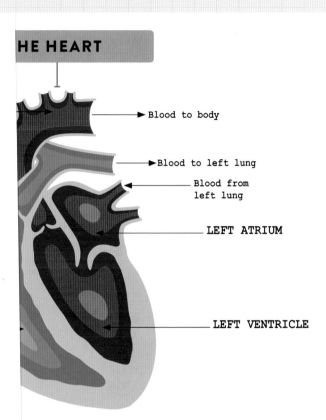

- Blood to body
- Blood to left lung
- Blood from left lung
- **LEFT ATRIUM**
- **LEFT VENTRICLE**

ide. When it beats, it pumps blood
flows through capillaries on the
s oxygen arriving with a new breath.
flows back into the heart's left side,
before being pushed out again by the next heartbeat. This time, the oxygenated
blood travels into the rest of the body and delivers supplies to organs and tissues.
As the blood moves around the body it starts to run out of oxygen—it is now
deoxygenated. Every time the heart beats, the oxygenated blood it pumps out
pushes the blood ahead of it farther through the blood vessels. Deoxygenated
blood eventually arrives back at the heart and the cycle begins again.

10.4 INSIDE THE MOUTH

The mouth is the very beginning of the digestive system—it's here that food enters your body and starts to get broken down. Solid food is too big to fit in your body straight away though, so the teeth have work to do before you can start digesting.

Teeth cut and crush food into smaller pieces, and saliva (spit) makes the pieces moist so they travel down the throat more easily. The tongue helps by moving food around the mouth while you chew and pushing it down when you swallow. Animals with different diets have different teeth, because each type of tooth is good at breaking down a particular type of food. As humans are omnivores (see page 166) and eat a wide variety of food, we have four types of teeth:

TYPES OF TEETH IN HUMANS

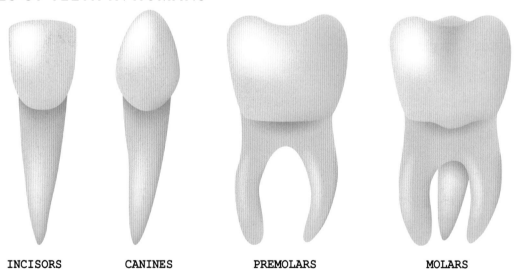

| INCISORS | CANINES | PREMOLARS | MOLARS |

1. **Incisors** The eight narrow rectangular teeth right at the front of your mouth cut food into pieces so it's easier to chew.
2. **Canines** The four pointy teeth in your mouth tear your food.
3. **Premolars** Next to each canine, these teeth have a flat surface for crushing food.
4. **Molars** Right at the back, these large flat teeth grind food down as you chew.

The first teeth you grow are called milk teeth, baby teeth, or primary teeth. They start developing inside the gums before a baby has even been born, but they don't show until about six months of age.

If you don't brush your teeth, a film of bacteria called plaque builds up. The bacteria feed on sugar in your food and produce acid that eats away at the enamel and forms painful holes, or cavities.

Structure of a tooth

As well as the part of a tooth you can see, there's a much longer part called the root that's hidden in your gum. Just like a plant's roots, this root anchors the tooth and stops it from falling out when you eat.

Right in the middle of a tooth is a soft substance called pulp, which holds blood vessels and nerves to bring nutrients and send messages between the teeth and the brain. A tough substance called dentin covers and protects the pulp, and above the gum they're both wrapped in a thick layer of an even harder material called enamel. The enamel is the part you can see and the part you brush—it's important to keep it healthy so it can keep doing its job and protect the inside of the tooth. Below the gum, cementum covers and protects the root.

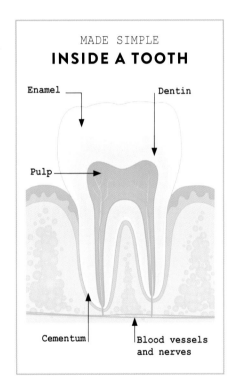

MADE SIMPLE
INSIDE A TOOTH

Enamel

Dentin

Pulp

Cementum

Blood vessels and nerves

ANSWER THIS

1. Which type of tooth tears food?

2. Why do humans have different types of teeth?

3. What does saliva do?

4. What is a cavity?

5. Where are a tooth's nerves and blood vessels?

10.5 THE DIGESTIVE SYSTEM

The digestive system is a collection of organs that break down your food into substances your body can use. Just chewing isn't enough; food goes through several stages inside the digestive system before it can be put to use.

After being swallowed, food moves down the esophagus to the stomach. Here stomach acid and chemicals called enzymes kill harmful microorganisms and churn the food into a paste. Once the stomach has done as much as it can, the partially digested food travels to the intestines, or gut, where most of the digestion takes place. The gut is made of two parts: the small intestine and the large intestine. Food arrives at the small intestine first, and more enzymes break it down into tiny molecules. Fully digested food molecules move out through the intestine wall into the bloodstream to be taken to cells around the body. Substances known as nutrients help the body to grow, repair, and generally keep working—these nutrients include fats, carbohydrates, proteins, and vitamins.

FACT

The large intestine is wider than the small intestine, but it's much shorter. The average adult's large intestine is 5 feet (1.5 meters) long, while the small intestine measures 23 feet (7 meters) from one end to the other—that's more than the height of a giraffe.

DIGESTIVE SYSTEM

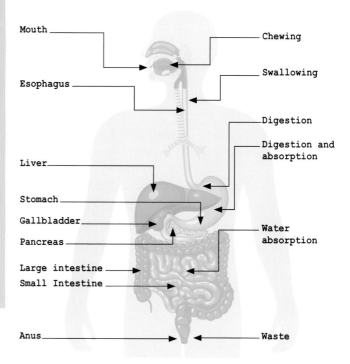

Mouth — Chewing

Esophagus — Swallowing

— Digestion

— Digestion and absorption

Liver

Stomach

Gallbladder — Water absorption

Pancreas

Large intestine

Small Intestine

Anus — Waste

Cells use oxygen and one particular carbohydrate—a sugar called glucose—to make energy. It's mostly waste—material the body can't digest or doesn't need—that reaches the large intestine. Any remaining water moves out through the wall to be used again, and the stuff that's left leaves the body through the anus as feces (poo).

The other organs

The stomach and intestines aren't the only organs in the digestive system. The pancreas produces enzymes, the chemicals that speed up digestion. The liver produces bile, a chemical that specifically targets and breaks down fat and oil. Bile and enzymes are stored in the gallbladder, a small pouch just under the liver, until a person eats and food begins to travel through the system.

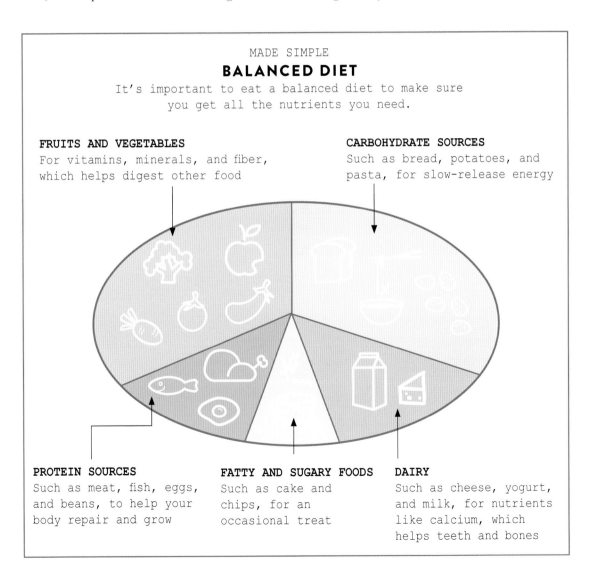

MADE SIMPLE
BALANCED DIET
It's important to eat a balanced diet to make sure you get all the nutrients you need.

FRUITS AND VEGETABLES
For vitamins, minerals, and fiber, which helps digest other food

CARBOHYDRATE SOURCES
Such as bread, potatoes, and pasta, for slow-release energy

PROTEIN SOURCES
Such as meat, fish, eggs, and beans, to help your body repair and grow

FATTY AND SUGARY FOODS
Such as cake and chips, for an occasional treat

DAIRY
Such as cheese, yogurt, and milk, for nutrients like calcium, which helps teeth and bones

10.6 THE IMMUNE SYSTEM

LESSON

Harmful bacteria and viruses can cause illness if they get into the body. You come into contact with millions of these germs every day, but they don't always make you sick. It's the job of the immune system to protect the body and keep it healthy.

Skin, eyelashes, scabs, and saliva all stop harmful microorganisms getting into the body, but if an invader (known as a pathogen) manages to sneak inside, the immune system leaps into action. The immune system is made up of organs and tissues including the lymph nodes, the spleen, the thymus, and the bone marrow. It produces several different types of cells that work together to fight off pathogens. One of the most important types is the white blood cell.

FACT

Vaccines are dead or altered pathogens that give people immunity against certain illnesses when they're injected or swallowed. The body doesn't know that the pathogens are harmless, so it develops defenses to stop the disease. If the disease ever attacks for real, the immune system knows how to quickly fight it off.

HUMAN IMMUNE SYSTEM

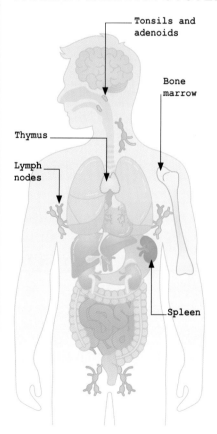

Tonsils and adenoids

Bone marrow

Thymus

Lymph nodes

Spleen

TONSILS AND ADENOIDS trap germs that enter through the nose and mouth.
THYMUS stores lymphocytes while they develop and mature.
BONE MARROW produces white blood cells.
LYMPH NODES make a watery liquid called lymph that transports germ-fighting cells.
SPLEEN stores white blood cells and detects pathogens in the blood.

Body defenders

White blood cells, or "leukocytes," patrol the body by moving through the huge network of blood vessels. If they come across anything that shouldn't be there, they send out an alarm signal and more cells rush over to help destroy it. There are two main types of white blood cells, each with a different role:

- **Phagocytes** These cells capture and absorb invaders (*phagein* means "to eat" in ancient Greek).
- **Lymphocytes** These cells remember all the pathogens that have been in the body before and how to get rid of them.

Some cells make structures called antibodies, which attach to a pathogen and stop it from causing any harm. They act like a sign, telling other cells to absorb and destroy the attacker. Every pathogen is a different shape, so the cells must make an antibody the right shape to lock on tightly. Antibodies stick around after the invader is gone, so the body doesn't have to work out how to make it all over again if the same disease comes back.

Babies are born with some immunity, as antibodies are passed from their mothers while they grow in the womb. The rest of a person's immune system develops as they go through life and encounter different pathogens—every time you're ill, your body learns and improves its defenses.

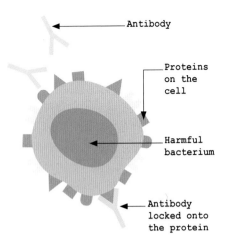

Antibody

Proteins on the cell

Harmful bacterium

Antibody locked onto the protein

INVADING PATHOGEN
Cells make antibodies that fit the shape of the pathogen.

ANSWER THIS

1. Where are white blood cells made?

2. Which type of white blood cell "eats" invaders?

3. Which structure attaches to pathogens?

4. What does the spleen do?

5. What is another name for white blood cells?

10.7 THE NERVOUS SYSTEM

Think about a time you were really happy. Now blink three times. Those might seem like simple things, but lots of messages had to be sent back and forth at high speed inside your body for you to understand and follow the instructions—this is the job of the nervous system.

NERVOUS SYSTEM

CENTRAL NERVOUS SYSTEM

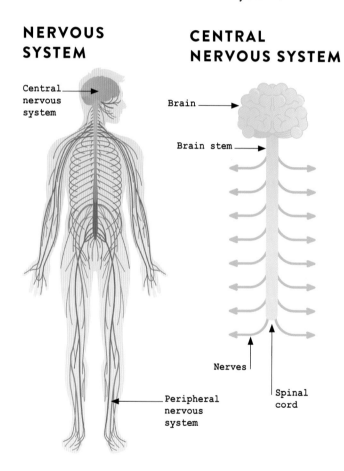

Central nervous system

Peripheral nervous system

Brain

Brain stem

Nerves

Spinal cord

Held safely inside the skull, the brain is the control center of the nervous system. It's a spongy gray organ that acts like a supercomputer, taking in information and sending messages to the rest of the body. It coordinates everything your body does, from blinking and breathing to singing and remembering to say happy birthday to a friend. The brain is made up of multiple parts, each with its own jobs to do.

At the base of the brain is the brain stem, which connects it to a long cable running all the way down the back. This is the spinal cord, which helps transport information between the brain and other body parts. The brain, the brain stem, and the spinal cord make up the central nervous system, but all their work would be for nothing without the nerves.

FACT No one really understands why we dream. Some scientists think it's the brain's way of making sense of all the information it receives: by playing out imaginary scenes it can work out which facts and feelings go together and decide what to store away as memories.

MAIN PARTS OF THE BRAIN

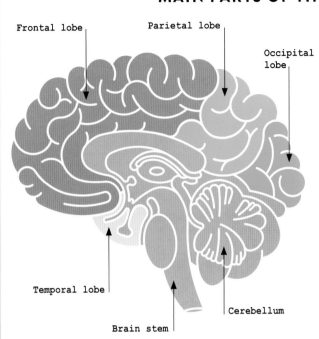

Frontal lobe

Parietal lobe

Occipital lobe

Temporal lobe

Brain stem

Cerebellum

FRONTAL LOBE
Speaking, problem solving, coordinating movement

TEMPORAL LOBE
Understanding sounds and language, storing memories

PARIETAL LOBE
Processing touch and taste, orienting the body

OCCIPITAL LOBE
Processing sight, working out size and distance

CEREBELLUM
Coordinating and balancing the body

BRAIN STEM
Controlling involuntary muscles, like the heart

Peripheral nervous system

The peripheral nervous system is the huge branching network of nerves running through the body. Nerves are thin fibers made from special cells called neurons, and they transport information as tiny pulses of electricity. Sensory receptors—structures like the eyes, tongue, and fingertips that sense the world around them—send messages up to the brain, and the brain sends back a reply or instruction. Signals travel at high speed along the nerves—think about how quickly you move your hand back when you touch something hot.

When the same set of messages travels back and forth multiple times, new nerve pathways are created and the structure of the nervous system changes slightly. This is how you learn; every time you practice something, your brain strengthens the paths so it gets better at controlling all the movements and thoughts involved.

ANSWER THIS

1. Which type of cell passes messages through the body?

2. What are the three parts of the central nervous system?

3. What protects the brain?

4. Which part of the brain stores memories?

5. The eyes and fingertips are examples of_____?

THE REPRODUCTIVE SYSTEM

Humans reproduce sexually, using special cells called gametes from two people. To make these cells and bring them together, males and females have different reproductive systems.

People are born with their reproductive systems already in place, but they don't start working for several years. Children cannot reproduce because their reproductive systems aren't fully developed. Between the ages of 8 and 14, they start to go through a series of changes known as puberty. Puberty is caused by the release of certain chemicals in the body and it leads to changes like growth spurts, body hair, voices breaking in boys, and the development of breasts in girls.

Puberty also sets off the menstrual cycle in females—a female who has started menstruating is able to get pregnant. During this cycle, the walls of the uterus thicken and an egg cell is released from one of the ovaries into an oviduct. If the egg does not meet a sperm, the uterus lining breaks down and causes bleeding known as a period.

THE REPRODUCTIVE ORGANS

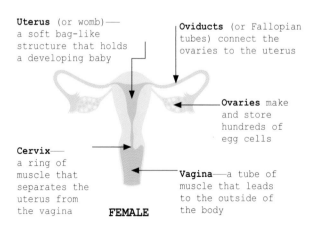

Uterus (or womb)— a soft bag-like structure that holds a developing baby

Oviducts (or Fallopian tubes) connect the ovaries to the uterus

Ovaries make and store hundreds of egg cells

Cervix— a ring of muscle that separates the uterus from the vagina

Vagina—a tube of muscle that leads to the outside of the body

FEMALE

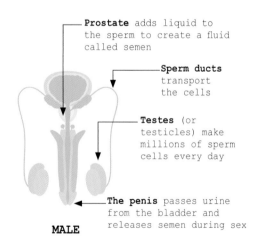

Prostate adds liquid to the sperm to create a fluid called semen

Sperm ducts transport the cells

Testes (or testicles) make millions of sperm cells every day

The penis passes urine from the bladder and releases semen during sex

MALE

FACT

Females have all their eggs from birth. At around the age of 50, they start to go through a process called menopause, where their periods stop and they become unable to get pregnant.

Pregnancy

Sometimes an egg cell does meet a sperm in the oviduct. This is usually because the female has had sex with a male and semen was released while the male's penis was inside the female's vagina. The fastest sperm swims up to the egg and the two cells combine their DNA (see page 174)—when this happens, the egg is described as fertilized and the female becomes pregnant.

The fertilized egg moves to the uterus and attaches to the thick lining. Here the cell splits in half again and again, growing into a baby over nine months. The developing baby is connected to its mother by a tube and receives oxygen and nutrients from the female's body. Once the baby is ready to be born, the cervix relaxes and muscles in the uterus push the baby out through the vagina.

ANSWER THIS

1. Where are sperm created?

2. How long does it take for a baby to develop?

3. What separates the uterus and the vagina?

4. Which two fluids come out of the penis?

5. What is the name for sex cells?

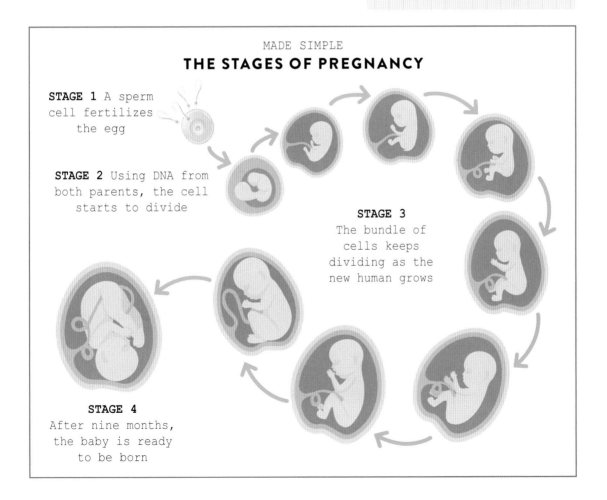

MADE SIMPLE
THE STAGES OF PREGNANCY

STAGE 1 A sperm cell fertilizes the egg

STAGE 2 Using DNA from both parents, the cell starts to divide

STAGE 3 The bundle of cells keeps dividing as the new human grows

STAGE 4 After nine months, the baby is ready to be born

THE HUMAN BODY

1. Which of these is not a function of the skeleton?
   a. Protecting soft organs
   b. Supporting the body
   c. Making new blood cells
   d. Transporting blood

2. What do the molar teeth do?
   a. Grind food
   b. Tear food
   c. Cut food
   d. Find food

3. Which gas is removed from the blood during respiration?
   a. Oxygen
   b. Methane
   c. Helium
   d. Carbon dioxide

4. Which blood vessels carry deoxygenated blood to the heart?
   a. Arteries
   b. Drains
   c. Veins
   d. Aorta

5. If you stretched out the small intestine it would be...
   a. as long as a whale
   b. as tall as a skyscraper
   c. as long as a bed
   d. as tall as a giraffe

6. Which system sends messages between the brain and the rest of the body?
   a. Circulatory system
   b. Nervous system
   c. Skeletal system
   d. Digestive system

7. Cells that can make a baby are called...
   a. Neurons
   b. Capillaries
   c. Proteins
   d. Gametes

8. What builds up on teeth if they're not brushed properly?
   a. Plaque
   b. Dentin
   c. Pulp
   d. Enamel

9. What is the name for an invader in the body?
   a. Antibody
   b. Pathogen
   c. Leukocyte
   d. Lymphocyte

10. How many different skeletal muscles are there?
    a. 450
    b. More than 600
    c. 800
    d. More than 1,000

Answers on page 216

SIMPLE SUMMARY

Your body is packed with organs and systems that each carry out their own important tasks, day and night.

- The skeleton supports the complex collection of tissues that work together to keep you alive. The adult human skeleton is made up from 206 bones.

- The end of each bone in a joint is covered with a smooth substance called cartilage and made slippery with a liquid called synovial fluid.

- There are more than 600 different skeletal muscles in the body.

- The respiratory system is a group of organs and tissues that supply all the cells in the body with the oxygen they need to turn food into energy.

- Blood carries important supplies like water, nutrients, and oxygen to the cells and takes away any waste they produce.

- The heart has four chambers, two on each side. When it beats, it pumps blood from its right side to the lungs.

- Teeth cut and crush food into smaller pieces, and saliva (spit) makes the pieces moist so they travel down the throat more easily.

- Food goes through several stages inside the digestive system.

- The immune system is made up of organs and tissues including the lymph nodes, the spleen, the thymus, and the bone marrow.

- The brain is the control center of the nervous system.

- Humans reproduce sexually, using special cells called gametes from two people.

QUIZ TIME

ANSWERS

LESSON 1

ANSWER THIS

1.1 Particles and Atoms
1. Proton
2. Electron
3. Shells
4. Nucleus
5. More

1.2 Chemical Elements
1. Over 90
2. Broken down into any other substances
3. Neon
4. The same

1.3 The Periodic Table
1. Electron shells
2. Dmitri Mendeleev
3. Group
4. Inert gases
5. Metal

1.4 Molecules and Compounds
1. No, it's a compound
2. Covalent and ionic
3. A molecule made of atoms of more than one element
4. Ionic
5. Molecular formula

1.5 Properties of Materials
1. The ability to soak up liquids
2. Could include ceramic, thin glass, or concrete
3. Ductility, conductivity, and durability
4. Opaque

1.7 Acids and Alkalis
1. Negative
2. Salt and water
3. Hand soap
4. Bitter
5. 1

QUIZ TIME
1. b.
2. c.
3. d.
4. c.
5. c.
6. b.
7. a.
8. b.
9. a.
10. b.

LESSON 2

ANSWER THIS

2.1 Wave Properties
1. Mechanical
2. Peak or crest
3. The position of the field or particle when it's not being vibrated
4. Transverse
5. From crest to crest

2.2 The Electromagnetic Spectrum

1. Gamma
2. Infrared
3. EM waves can move through a vacuum
4. Ultraviolet (UV)

2.3 Visible Light

1. Speed and direction
2. Opaque
3. Retina
4. Optic nerve

2.4 Color

1. Red
2. Dispersion
3. Color blindness
4. Black

2.5 X-rays

1. 1895
2. Children could suffer from burned skin and have a higher chance of getting cancer
3. Bones
4. They can look inside objects without breaking them open

2.6 Radio Waves

1. Because their wavelengths are so long
2. Radio waves from outer space
3. Wireless adapter
4. Radio detection and ranging

2.7 Sound

1. Cochlea
2. Pinna
3. Amplitude
4. Higher
5. The eruption of Krakatoa

2.8 Ultrasound and Infrasound

1. Dogs, cats, mice, dolphins, bush babies, or bats
2. Returning echoes/ reflected sound waves
3. To check the health of their baby
4. Water depth
5. 20 Hz

QUIZ TIME

1. c.
2. b.
3. d.
4. a.
5. d.
6. b.
7. a.
8. b.
9. c.
10. a.

LESSON 3

ANSWER THIS

3.1 The Universe and the Galaxy

1. Spiral
2. The big bang
3. 380,000 years after the big bang
4. 100,000 light-years
5. 1

3.2 Comets, Asteroids, and Meteors

1. Coma
2. 200 years
3. When it lands on Earth
4. Between Mars and Jupiter

3.4 The Solar System

1. Gas giant
2. Uranus
3. Mercury
4. 889 million miles

3.5 Earth's Orbit

1. Elliptical
2. Winter
3. 23.5°
4. 67,000 miles an hour

3.6 Day and Night

1. West to east
2. Summer
3. 24
4. The poles

3.7 The Moon

1. Because it reflects light from the Sun
2. High tide
3. Eight
4. Because the Moon turns as it orbits Earth

3.8 Humans in Space

1. United States & USSR
2. 1969
3. As big as a football field
4. Third
5. Mars

QUIZ TIME

1. c.
2. d.
3. b.
4. d.
5. a.
6. c.
7. a.
8. b.
9. a.
10. d.

LESSON 4

ANSWER THIS

4.1 Formation of the Earth

1. 3.8 billion years ago
2. 1,240 miles (2,000 km) thick
3. The Moon
4. Iron and nickel
5. The mantle

4.2 Earth's Atmosphere

1. Five
2. Exosphere
3. UV rays
4. 78 percent

4.3 Tectonics

1. Convection currents in the mantle
2. Continental and oceanic
3. Constructive or divergent
4. Oceanic
5. 175 million years ago

4.4 Volcanos and Earthquakes

1. 2,282°F (1,250°C)
2. Moment Magnitude Scale
3. No
4. Lahar
5. The Ring of Fire

4.5 Rocks and Minerals

1. Sedimentary
2. Extrusive
3. Minerals
4. Obsidian
5. Sediment

4.6 Weathering

1. Soft rock
2. The roots
3. Sulfur dioxide
4. They expand
5. Erosion

4.7 The Water Cycle

1. Water falling from the sky
2. More than 4 billion years
3. Water vapor
4. Heat from the Sun
5. The hydrologic cycle

4.8 Weather and Climate

1. Meteorologists
2. The weather
3. Land
4. Heat
5. Carbon dioxide and methane

QUIZ TIME

1. c.
2. c.
3. c.
4. a.
5. d.
6. b.
7. a.
8. b.
9. c.
10. b.

LESSON 5

ANSWER THIS

5.1 What is a Force?
1. Newtons
2. Applied and action-at-a-distance
3. Pairs
4. Could include opening a door, picking something up, pushing a trolley, etc.

5.3 Gravity and Weight
1. Its mass and its distance from other objects
2. 38 pounds (17 kg)
3. Jupiter
4. 1687

5.4 Friction and Resistance
1. Opposite
2. Rough or uneven
3. Drag
4. Heat
5. Streamlined

5.5 Torque and Torsion
1. Moment
2. Applied
3. Pivot
4. Angular

5.6 Stretching, Squashing, and Bending
1. Deformation
2. Compression
3. It would triple
4. Robert Hooke
5. Flexible, elastic, and pliable

5.7 Upthrust
1. Sink
2. Weight and density
3. They have a low density and a wide surface for upthrust to act on
4. Archimedes
5. The volume of the submerged object

5.8 Pressure
1. Pascals
2. Higher
3. State
4. Air pressure
5. Solid

5.9 Magnets
1. Attract
2. Action-at-a-distance
3. Magnetar

QUIZ TIME
1. b.
2. a.
3. c.
4. a.
5. a.
6. d.
7. d.
8. b.
9. c.

LESSON 6

ANSWER THIS

6.1 Types of Energy
1. Elastic
2. Joules
3. Gravitational potential
4. Created or destroyed

6.2 Energy Transfer
1. Electrical transfer
2. Equal
3. Sankey diagram
4. Medium

6.3 Heating
1. Higher
2. Thermal energy
3. Convection

6.4 Combustion

1. Heat, light, carbon dioxide, and water
2. Heat
3. Exothermic
4. Color or smell

6.5 Electricity

1. Amperes (amps)
2. High to low
3. Insulator
4. Resistance

6.6 Electrical Circuits

1. To prevent electric shocks
2. Connect
3. Bulb or buzzer
4. Parallel

6.7 Electricity in the Home

1. Generator
2. Turn off the lights
3. Step-up transformer
4. To make it safe for use
5. Less water needs to be heated

6.8 Renewable and Nonrenewable Energy

1. The remains of dead plants and animals
2. Replaced
3. Hydroelectric power
4. Atoms

QUIZ TIME

1. d.
2. a.
3. b.
4. d.
5. b.
6. a.
7. d.
8. b.
9. c.
10. c.

LESSON 7

ANSWER THIS

7.2 Density

1. Density = Mass ÷ Volume
2. Gas
3. Temperature and pressure
4. Hydrogen bond
5. Water

7.3 Diffusion

1. Because the particles are held in place and can't move
2. Low
3. Spread out

7.4 Freezing and Melting

1. 32°F (0°C)
2. Slows down
3. None
4. Changes that can't be undone
5. Liquid

7.5 Boiling, Evaporation, and Condensation

1. Vaporization
2. At the surface
3. 212°F (100°C)
4. Evaporation

7.6 Sublimation and Deposition

1. On a high mountain
2. Liquid
3. Dry ice
4. Deposition

QUIZ TIME

1. c.
2. a.
3. c.
4. d.
5. c.
6. a.
7. b.
8. d.
9. a.
10. b.

LESSON 8

ANSWER THIS

8.1 Building Blocks of Life

1. Cell wall, vacuole, and chloroplast
2. In the nucleus
3. Over 30 trillion
4. Stem cells

8.2 Organizing Organisms

1. A species
2. The naming and grouping of species
3. So they can be used around the world

8.3 Microorganisms

1. Virus
2. To stop germs from entering your body
3. Inside another organism's cell
4. Yeast

8.4 Plants

1. Almost 400,000
2. Sunlight, water, and carbon dioxide
3. Through small holes called stomata
4. It produces oxygen that we breathe

8.5 Animals

1. Vertebrates have a backbone
2. About 97 percent
3. Body temperature changes with the surrounding temperature
4. Mammals

8.6 Habitats and Ecosystems

1. Food, a home, and a chance to reproduce
2. A microhabitat
3. Abiotic

8.7 Earth's Biomes

1. The layer of Earth where life exists
2. Tundra
3. Near the equator
4. Two
5. Temperate forest

8.8 Biodiversity

1. About 8.7 million
2. Human activity
3. 36
4. 80 percent

8.9 Food Chains and Webs

1. A producer/plant
2. Apex predator
3. Herbivore
4. An animal that eats both plants and other animals
5. Break down the bodies of dead organisms

QUIZ TIME

1. c.
2. b.
3. d.
4. a.
5. c.
6. a.
7. c.
8. d.
9. d.
10. a.

LESSON 9

ANSWER THIS

9.1 DNA

1. Adenine, cytosine, guanine, and thymine
2. Double helix
3. Allele
4. 23

9.3 Evolution

1. Charles Darwin
2. Individuals with certain genes/traits are more likely to survive and reproduce
3. Differences
4. Larger, longer
5. No, only a species can evolve

9.5 Competition

1. Intraspecific
2. Intraspecific
3. Cooperate
4. Resources

9.8 Fossils

1. Sedimentary
2. Soft parts
3. Paleontologists
4. By movements in the Earth's crust
5. Layers

1. d.
2. b.
3. d.
4. a.
5. d.
6. b.
7. a.
8. c.
9. c.
10. d.

LESSON 10

ANSWER THIS

10.1 The Skeleton and Muscles

1. 206
2. Skeletal, cardiac, and smooth
3. Synovial fluid
4. Relaxes
5. Ligament

10.2 The Respiratory System

1. Oxygen and glucose
2. Red blood cell
3. Carbon dioxide
4. It gives less energy and produces lactic acid
5. Energy

10.3 The Circulatory System

1. Form blood clots and scabs
2. Arteries
3. Oxygen
4. In the bone marrow

10.4 Inside the Mouth

1. Canines
2. Because they're omnivores
3. Makes food moist
4. A hole in the enamel
5. In the pulp

10.6 The Immune System

1. In the bone marrow
2. Phagocyte
3. Antibodies
4. Stores white blood cells and detects pathogens in the blood
5. Leukocytes

10.7 The Nervous System

1. Neuron
2. Brain, brain stem, and spinal cord
3. The skull
4. The temporal lobe
5. Sensory receptors

10.8 The Reproductive System

1. In the testes or testicles
2. Nine months
3. The cervix
4. Urine and semen
5. Gametes

QUIZ TIME

1. d.
2. a.
3. d.
4. c.
5. d.
6. b.
7. d.
8. a.
9. b.
10. b.

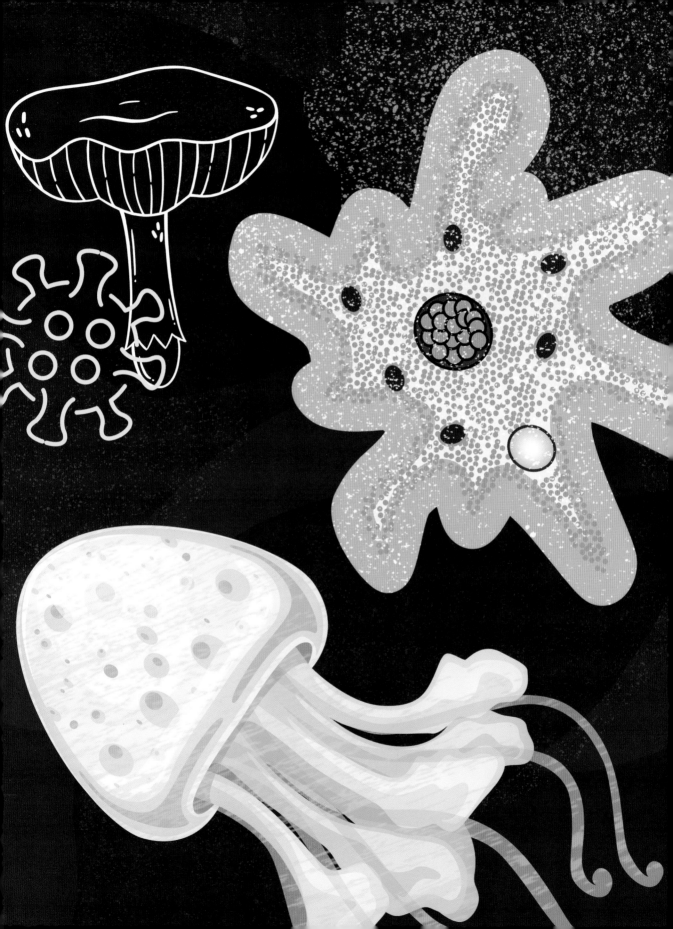

GLOSSARY

Alleles — Different versions of a particular gene.

Atmosphere — Layers of gas surrounding a planet.

Atom — Tiny unit of matter that makes up everything in the universe.

Biodiversity — The variety of living things in a particular area.

Chemical reaction — Process in which atoms in molecules break apart and rearrange to create new substances.

Combustion — Burning; a reaction that turns stored energy into light and heat.

Consumer — Organism that eats other organisms in a food chain or web.

Electron — Negatively charged subatomic particle that orbits an atom.

Element — Substance made up of only one type of atom, impossible to break down into other substances.

Energy — The ability of an object or system to do work, usually measured in joules.

Evolution — Changes in a species over a long period of time.

Galaxy — Group of millions or billions of stars (along with gas and space dust), all held together by gravity.

Immunity — The ability of an organism to protect itself against harmful microorganisms.

Mantle — The partly molten layer of the Earth that lies below the crust.

Matter — Any substance that has mass and takes up space.

Nucleus — The core of an atom containing the protons or neutrons, or the part of a cell that stores information and controls what it does.

Organism — An individual living thing.

pH scale — A scale from 1–14 that measures how acidic or alkaline substances are.

Precipitation — Water falling from the sky to the ground—rain, snow, sleet, and hail.

Wave — Disturbance in space and/or matter that causes a transfer of energy.

FURTHER READING

BOOKS:

100 Scientists Who Made History
Andrea Mills
DK Children, 2018

100 Steps for Science: Why It Works and How It Happened
Lisa Jane Gillespie
Wide Eyed Editions, 2017

Absolute Expert: Volcanoes
Lela Nargi
National Geographic Children's Books, 2018

Absolutely Everything!: A History of Earth, Dinosaurs, Rulers, Robots, and Other Things Too Numerous to Mention
Christopher Lloyd
What On Earth Books, 2018

Awesome Physics Experiments for Kids: 40 Fun Science Projects and Why They Work
Erica L. Colón
Rockridge Press, 2019

Big Questions from Little People: And Simple Answers from Great Minds
Gemma Elwin Harris
Ecco, 2012

Curiositree: Natural World: A Visual Compendium of Wonders from Nature
A.J. Wood
Wide Eyed Editions, 2016

Energy Lab for Kids: 40 Exciting Experiments to Explore, Create, Harness, and Unleash Energy
Emily Hawbaker
Quarry Books, 2017

Explanatorium of Science
DK and Smithsonian Institution
DK Children, 2019

Human Body!
DK and Smithsonian Institution
DK Children, 2019

It's So Amazing!: A Book about Eggs, Sperm, Birth, Babies, and Families
Robie H. Harris
Candlewick Press, 2014

Real Chemistry Experiments: 40 Exciting STEAM Activities for Kids
Edward P. Zovinka
Rockridge Press, 2019

Stupendous Science
Rob Beattie
QED Publishing, 2017

The Element in the Room:
Investigating the Atomic Ingredients
that Make Up Your Home
Mike Barfield
Laurence King Publishing, 2018

The Rocking Book of Rocks: An
Illustrated Guide to Everything Rocks,
Gems, and Minerals
Amy Ball & Florence Bullough
Wide Eyed Editions, 2019

The Ultimate Book of Planet Earth
Anne-Sophie Baumann
Twirl, 2019

The Usborne Official Astronaut's
Handbook
Louie Stowell
Usborne, 2015

Weather in 30 Seconds: 30 Amazing
Topics for Weather Whizz Kids
Explained in Half a Minute
Jen Green
Ivy Kids, 2017

When the Whales Walked: And Other
Incredible Evolutionary Journeys
Dougal Dixon
Words and Pictures, 2018

Why?: Over 1,111 Answers to
Everything
Crispin Boyer
National Geographic Children's Books,
2015

WEBSITES:
BrainPOP
www.brainpop.com/science

Climate Kids
www.climatekids.nasa.gov

Crash Course Kids
www.youtube.com/crashcoursekids

Frontiers for Young Minds
kids.frontiersin.org

NASA Kids' Club
www.nasa.gov/kidsclub

INDEX

hydrogen 14, 54, 70, 135
hydrogen ions 24, 25
hydrosphere 82
hydroxide ions 24, 25

I
ice 135, 138, 142, 145
immune system 202–203
inertia 92
infrared 32, 117
infrasound 45
inheritance 174–175
insulators, electrical 121
invertebrates 158, 159

J
joints 193
Jupiter 53, 57, 58, 95

L
laws of motion 90, 91, 93
leap years 58
light waves 33, 34–35, 112, 113
light-years 50
Linnaean classification 152–153
liquid diffusion 136–137
liquids 24, 132, 133, 136, 139
longitudinal waves 30

M
magnets 106–107
Mars 53, 56, 58, 65, 95
mass extinctions 184, 185
material properties 20–21
matter 132–133
mechanical waves 30
melting points 138, 139
Mercury 53, 56, 58, 59, 95
meteors 53, 71
microhabitats 160
microorganisms 154–155, 160
microwaves 32
minerals 78
mixtures 144
molecules 18–19
Moon 58, 62–63, 70, 95
motion 92–93
motion sickness 92
mouths 198–199
muscles 193

N
natural selection 176
neon 15, 72
Neptune 57, 58, 95

nervous systems 204–205
neutralization 25
neutrons 12, 13
Newton, Isaac 90, 93, 94
nights 60
nonrenewable energy 126, 127
North Pole 59, 60, 107, 162

O
organisms 152–153
oxygen 14, 18
    in atmosphere 72
    in human body 137, 194, 195, 196, 197
    in photosynthesis 157
    role in combustion 25, 118, 119
ozone layer 72

P
particles 12–13
periodic tables 16–17
pH scales 25
photosynthesis 115, 157
pitch 45
planets 56–57
plants 83, 150, 156–157, 179, 180
precipitation 82, 83
pregnancy 207
pressure 104–105, 133, 134
protons 12, 13

R
radiation 114, 115, 117
radio waves 32, 40–41
rainbow spectrum 36, 37
reflection 35
refraction 34, 35
renewable energy 126, 127
replacement 23
reproductive systems 206–207
resistance 97
respiratory system 194–195
rocks 78–81, 104

S
Sankey diagram 115
Saturn 57, 58, 95
seasons 59, 61
selective breeding 182–183
sexual reproduction 206, 207
skeletons 192–193
solar systems 50, 56–57, 58
solids 132, 133
solutions 144–145
sound waves 42–45, 112, 113

South Pole 59, 60, 107, 162
space travel 64–65
squashing forces 100, 101
stars 54–55, 106
static electricity 120
stem cells 150
stretching forces 100, 101
sublimation 133, 142
Sun 54, 56, 58, 59, 60, 61
synthesis 23

T
tectonic plates 74–75
teeth, human 198–199
temperature 116, 134
thermal energy 116
tides 63
time zones 60, 61
torque 98, 99
torsion 98, 99
transpiration 83
transverse waves 30

U
ultrasound 44
ultraviolet 33
unbalanced forces 91
universe 50–51
upthrust 102–103
Uranus 57, 58, 95

V
vaccination 202
Venus 53, 56, 58, 60, 95
vertebrates 158
vibrations 112
viruses 153, 202
visible light 33, 34–35, 112, 113
volcanoes 76–77

W
water 18, 82–83, 135, 138
water cycle 82–83
wave properties 30–31
weather 84–85
weathering 80–81
weight 95
wind 84

X
X-rays 33, 38–39

Y
years 58, 59

CREDITS

Mum and Dad—May May did it! Thank you for encouraging my love of books and showing me how fascinating the world is, and for all your love and support. Bean—thank you for keeping me fed and reminding me to sleep. Thanks for having more belief in me than I do in myself. You are an exceptionally good egg. And to all those who have helped me and taken chances on me in the first years of my career—thank you, thank you, thank you.

Images:
Unless otherwise noted, all images have been created by Tall Tree.

Shutterstock: 9, 27, 47, 66, 86, 108, 128, 146, 168, 188, 208, 210 Blan-k; 13 snapgalleria; 15 oorka; Nowik Sylwia, iaRada, angkrit; 16–17 stockshoppe; 18 stihii; 18, 55, 58, 62, 193 Nasky; 19, 33, 64, 79, 132, 134, 154, 195, 202, 204 VectorMine; 21 kup1984, shaineast, moj0j0, FARBAI; Siberian Photographer, Roaddesign, Made by Marko; Ilya Bolotov, KittyVector, Tomacco; 24–25 BlueRingMedia; 32–33 brgfx; 35, 106 CRStocker; 36, 43, 77, 101 udaix; 37 Fouad A. Saad; 39 Alexander_P; 40 Pensiri, dymentyd, msr meloool; 41 fad82, Maksym Drozd; 42 Pretty Vectors; 45 Maquiladora, KBel; 50, 60, 61, 76, 137, 155, 163, 194 Designua; 51 robuart; 53, 56, 57, 95 D1 min; 58 Nasky; 59 shooarts; 62 Nevada31; 63 annalisa e marina durante; 73 Inna Bigun, pingebat; 80 Glasscage; 81 MicroOne, Vectors Bang; 82–83 Merkushev Vasiliy; 84 Ziablik; 90 aarrows, NiklsN; 91 Vladimir Sviracevic; 92 autovector, Bohdana Seheda, Rauf Aliyev, Julia Babii; 93 Slobodan Djajic, Great_Kit, Fidan Farajullayeva; 96 Designua, GoTaR; 97 NotionPic, sportpoint, nubephoto; 98 paw; 99 Lilia03; 105 angkrit; 107 Milagli; 113 etraveler, Bika Ambon, Titov Nikolai, VikiVector, Supza, Yakan; Jo Karen, Panda Vector; 114 justone, AVIcon, Strejman, Studio_G, newelle, Irene Ziegler, notbad; 115 NartGraphic; 116 OSweetNature; 117 T VECTOR ICONS, VikiVector; 120 KittyVector; 121 Ilya Bolotov, Edilus, Vector Dude, Elena Tryapitsyna; Maike Hildebrandt, Sudowoodo, ONYXprj, oculo; 122 Webspark; 123 ducu59us; 124 VoodooDot, GzP_Design, Strejman; 125 Macrovector, Miuky; 127 mjaud, (hydroelectric image) VoodooDot, Shanvood; 133 MicroOne; 135 Andrii Symonenko; 136 gritsalak karalak; 138 KlaraDo; stockakia; 139 kilkavbanke; 141 knahthra, Jane Kelly, YummyBuum, Irina Shatilova, Inna Bigun; 143 Tolpeeva Nadezda; 144 oorka; 145 Solar, Garia, Ivan Feoktistov; 150, 151 Steve Cymro; 152 Panda Vector, Kazakova Maryia; 153 Rhoeo, Spreadthesign, Panda Vector, Park Ji Sun, Platonova Sveta; 156 Kazakova Maryia; 157 Jakinnboaz; 158 Vecton; 159 Part of Design, Vecton, KOSTENKO3, Spreadthesign, NotionPic, SaveJungle; 161 Panda Vector, Spreadthesign, davooda; 164 bsd, Decent, Jacky Co, Kozinn91; 165 Lemberg Vector studio, Webspark, Rvector, CNuisin; 167 Baurz1973; 172 Fancy Tapis; 173 Emre Terim; 174 yayha; 175 ANNA_KOVA, Vector_dream_team, csn.y; 177 Aldona Griskeviciene; 179 Semiankova Inha, GraphicsRF; 181 iana kauri, MelnikPave; 182–183 pale62, Hennadii H, tcheres, Airin.dizain, super icon, archivector, cammep, DenysHolovatiuk; 185 alinabel; 187 stihii and edited by Sarah Skeate; 192 stihii; 193, 197, 200, 206 Olga Bolbot; 196 Pawel Graczyk; 198 gritsalak karalak; 199 Marochkina Anastasiia; 201 nnnnae; 205 shopplaywood; 207 BlueRingMedia, Shanvood.